FOUR

SEASONS

of

LEADERSHIP

DAVID NEIDERT

#41586193

For permissions requests, or additional information, please contact the publisher at:

Executive Excellence Publishing
1344 East 1120 South
Provo, UT 84606
phone: 1-801-377-4060
fax: 1-801-377-5960
website: www.eep.com

Printed in the United States

10 9 8 7 6 5 4 3 2 1

ISBN 1-890009-56-3

Cover design by Ginger McGovern
Printed by Publishers Press

Dedication

"To the Seven, I am becoming authentic only with them—God, Rhonda, Sarah, David, Mariah, Damon & Phoenix."

Acknowledgement

THERE IS ONE FACT I KNOW WITH CERTAINTY; I have been significantly influenced by a multitude of people throughout my life. This book is merely an expression of the mark they have all left on me. While I could never recount everyone who crossed my path, I want to thank those that influenced my personal growth and the writing of *Four Seasons of Leadership*.

I am deeply grateful to the staff of Executive Excellence Publishing for seeing promise in this manuscript. I am also grateful they were willing to take a risk with me. Thus a special thanks to Ken Shelton and Trent Price.

I must also acknowledge the prominent place the International Management Council of the YMCA plays in my leadership development. I could not have learned leadership or written about it without the support of Jodeen Sterba, Don Kyzer, Dan Sager, Division IV members, and my national friends. Thank you for trusting me and sharing the vision of this organization.

I am equally appreciative to my staff at Anderson University. They make practicing leadership a joy. Thanks Patty, Carol, Carolyn, Marlew, Regina, Diane, Paula, Les, Randy and students. Anderson University is indeed an institution that provides an environment for professional growth, teaching opportunities, and challenging personal reflection. While no organization is a utopia, Anderson University is truly an institution that nurtures and loves its members. To everyone at Anderson University, past and current, thank you for believing in me.

Thanks also to the Institute of Certified Professional Managers, the Anderson Area Leadership Academy and their staffs for allowing me to absorb the lessons of servanthood. And to those that endorsed this book, thanks for taking the time to read it in the early stages. Your belief, encouragement, and critique are priceless.

I must finally thank those closest to me. Without them, I would not be unfolding as I was created to be. My deepest appreciation and love are given to my parents, brother and sister, and their families, and also to Gustav and Aletta Jeeninga, Bobbette Snyder, Dirk Johnson who has passed from this sphere, my church family and pastors. And last, my love and appreciation to those to whom this book is dedicated. Thank you for making our house a home.

There is one fact I know with certainty; I have been significantly influenced by a multitude of people throughout my life. Thank you all for blessing me with your lives and bringing *Four Seasons of Leadership* into existence.

Table of Contents

Introduction to
The Four Seasons
of Leadership

THERE ARE NO QUICK FIXES. While we dream there are easy paths or hope we will find the genie to make our wishes come true, the reality is that hard work, action and perseverance are the only "fairy dust" that will fulfill our dreams.

This book is about fulfilling your leadership and life dreams. It is written to help you consider your life and legacy. By careful and diligent reading, you will begin to see your dreams unfold and your life work start to take shape.

This book is divided into four sections—Winter, Spring, Summer and Autumn—to correspond with the seasons of the year. Just like the cycle of life on this planet, so we each need a Season to understand who we are, why we are here, what we are doing and how we can make a difference in this world.

The four sections described in this book represent learning times in your journey to leadership. The Winter Season relates to self-introspection, creating a mission statement and setting goals. The Spring Season is about learning from your mistakes, formal education and taking the risks necessary to reach your goals. In the Summer Season, you will explore building a balanced life and relationships through the readings and questions. Finally, all the preparation will come together as you explore leadership and life skills in the Autumn Season. It is in this season that all the work of Winter, Spring and Summer will have their culmination.

Within each Season, you will encounter twenty-two individual thought units. Each unit presents a specific quality, skill or idea essential to your leadership development. At the end of each unit I list several questions and action items. These are designed to focus your study and to help you move toward application of the principles and skills you are reading. I suggest working through the units steadily one or two at a time. This pace will help you maintain a continuity in your studies, while giving each unit the attention it requires in order to internalize its message.

In addition to the thought units, at the beginning of each Season is a recommended list of books for reading. There are three—sometimes four—books for each Season. The suggestion is reading one book every month over the coming year. These books are recommended to assist you in understanding the various seasons of your development. These books will invite you to discover your potential and shape your future.

My children, now grown, loved to read with my wife and me as they readied for bed. One of our favorite books was a simple tale of two friends, Frog and Toad, written by Arnold Lobel. While a fanciful story of two amphibious friends, it contains for us a reminder of planting, tending and nurturing the seeds of leadership and purpose so necessary for our fulfillment as human beings.

In the story of The Garden, Toad desires to have a garden as beautiful as his friend Frog. Toad, wishing he too had a garden, accepts the seeds Frog gives him but misses the words about hard work and patience. In Toad's excitement, he throws the seeds on the ground and yells, "Now seeds, start growing!" When the seeds do not immediately grow, Toad uses the techniques of shouting, reading stories and poetry, and singing songs to his garden. Yet, alas, the seeds planted in haste and excitement do not immediately sprout.

In exhaustion, bewilderment and frustration, Toad falls asleep. But a miraculous event happens during Toad's slumber, the seeds begin to grow. As Frog happens by, he declares to Toad, "Look at your garden!" To Toad's amazement, the seeds are growing and peeking through the surface of the soil. As Toad wipes his forehead with his handkerchief, he comments with a sigh, "You were right Frog, gardening is very hard work!"

We are often just like Toad in our leadership search. We believe that amassing books, tapes and a plethora of seminar hours will build for us a beautiful garden of leadership and purpose. Seeing the success of others, we, too, imagine a beautiful garden will grow for us as well if we only throw a few seeds on our soil. And if that does not work, we will try some new technique or latest fad to get us to our idealized life.

But what we fail to realize is that building a beautiful life or legacy of leadership takes hard work. The building of a garden will require us to get our hands dirty, tend to what we are sowing, and watch diligently for the qualities of leadership and purpose to take root in us. No amount of yelling or encouragement or reading or education will cause the seeds of leadership to automatically grow. It is only through tending for a Season, living principles, and working very hard that the seeds of a full life will become a reality.

There are no quick fixes. Only perseverance, determination and hard work will bring fruit to your endeavors. I trust you will accept my invitation to find an abundant life as you journey through these Seasons.

David Neidert
Anderson, Indiana
1999

WINTER
S E A S O N

WINTER **IS A WONDERFUL SEASON.** While we often dislike the cold days, long nights and apparent bleakness, we forget it is a time of rest and renewal. The earth, in this season, takes time to regenerate itself, lying dormant with the full intent of coming alive in the warmer months. This time of regeneration is a necessary piece of the life cycle. It is during these weeks that nutrients and minerals are restored to the ground, waiting to provide nourishment for the growing seasons. Winter is a time of hope for the earth—one in which it believes the renewal will bear fruit in its own time.

As potential leaders, we also need a time of renewal and reflection. Often we are caught in the trap of activity without considering if those actions are the right ones for our lives, organizations or communities. With little or no forethought, we accept what life delivers—day in and day out. The problem is we may end up where we never intended or wanted to be at the conclusion of life's journey. For many that moment is filled with regret and a sense of being unfinished.

This section is titled The Winter Season for that very reason. The following pages invite you to consider in detail your life mission and purpose, goals, and the passion you have for making your dreams realities. It is a time for renewal and building a foundation for the remaining seasons of your life. If your work in this season is diligent, it will provide the nutrients for your future.

While it may seem tedious and slow going, it is important that you work diligently through the pages that follow. This pace will provide you with a solid foundation because you have taken the time to know exactly what you want to accomplish in life. Working carefully in the Winter Season will reap bountiful dividends in your actions if they are focused, purposeful and right for you.

The need for reflection has been central to some of the world's greatest leaders. Gandhi, Mohammed, Susan B. Anthony, Martin Luther King and the Apostle Paul are just a few who spent a Winter Season coming to understand their life purpose and calling. Out of this season of life, they sprang with passion and purpose that changed the world. While you may not transform the world, you will transform yourself as you spend time in the Winter. And who knows, you may indeed emerge with a purpose and energy that will move mountains.

RECOMMENDED BOOKS FOR THE WINTER SEASON:
Man's Search for Meaning. Victor E. Frankl. Beacon Press: Boston. 1992

Servant Leadership: A Journey Into The Nature Of Legitimate Power And Greatness. Robert K. Greenleaf. Paulist Press: New York. 1977

Principle Centered Leadership. Stephen Covey. Summit Books: New York. 1991

Your Life Purpose

I know the plans I have for you,
declares the Lord, plans to prosper you and
not to harm you, plans to give you hope and
a future.

—Jeremiah, the Prophet
The Bible, Jeremiah 29:11

HAVE YOU EVER CONSIDERED there is a reason for your existence? Have you ever wondered if there is an under-taking meant just for you?

Growing an effective leadership and life legacy starts when you recognize there is a calling laying dormant in your heart. One of the most defining moments for any human being is identifying that special purpose that is buried deep within them. Once discerned, it is that special sense of pur-pose which drives a person's life toward true fulfillment, whether it be to historical prominence or making a home a place of joy and peace.

We live in a historical moment that is fixated on the characteristics of the "Great Leader." Scholars' research and hungry audiences devour the latest information on the traits of great leadership in an attempt to find the single kernel of inspiration that will assist them in identifying their own leadership capacity.

But knowing the characteristics of another person does not necessarily help you to identify the purpose for your own life. More important than a list of qualities about another person is knowing your own purpose and passion for your existence. There is a seed of purpose awaiting your recognition.

I had the opportunity to visit the Holocaust Museum in Jerusalem during a recent trip. While there, I took a reflective stroll through the Garden of Remembrance. In this garden are trees planted for any person who helped save a Jew during WW II. It is a peaceful and humbling place where hundreds of names appear on small, black plaques next to trees. Oskar Schindler is buried here as a tribute to his courage in saving just one human life at a time.

When I returned to the States, I recounted this humbling experience with a friend. During our conversation, I reflected, "You know, out of fear people often do things that are not right. I know some of my family were imprisoned during World War II, but I wonder if my Hungarian ancestry helped or hurt Jews?" With deep insight, my friend replied, "Did you ever consider maybe you are here for changing whatever happened in the past?"

Realizing your purpose for being here begins the transformation of your life. We are all here for a reason. You have a purpose for being here. The most fulfilling moment will come when you know what it is.

• "What is calling you in life? Is it a sense of injustice, the need for self-identity or recognition, or a desire to leave some life legacy?

• What is in your heart, that when you speak about it, your heart pumps and the passion in your voice becomes noticeable to yourself and others?

• What is it that deeply stirs you emotionally when you encounter it in your world or in the larger context of society?

• What do you long to do in your life when the noise of the crowds and the busyness of the day fade into the darkness, leaving you alone with your own thoughts?

What Are You Waiting For?

As for man, his days are like grass, he flourishes like a flower of the field; then a scorching desert wind blows over it and it is gone; and its place remembers it no more.

—A Song of David
The Bible, Psalms 103:15

FROM ANCIENT STORIES like the Babylonian Gilgamesh Epic to the Death of a Salesman, all humanity has wrestled with the meaning of life. All religions admonish their disciples to seek the answers to these questions in order to find peace in their souls. Many seek in conventional ways to fill the vacuum of their spirit, while others pursue unorthodox methods to fill the void of their inner being. Yet with all this searching, one cruel fact is played out daily at numerous deathbeds, I wish I could have. . . .

Leaving a life or leadership legacy starts with answering questions that reveal the deepest meaning for our existence. Growing out of your sense of calling or purpose is a realization that your direction, energies and actions are rooted in how you live your life daily. Why is it that people always wait for retirement to consider what they should be doing with their life, leadership, expertise or time? Over a career spanning 40 or 50 years, they keep dreaming about a better life or doing what they have always desired to undertake. And in the meantime, they live a life of quiet desperation. What are we saving ourselves for?

When you come to the end of life, you should be used up. There is no interest accumulation or stock dividend for the days of your life. Effective people know it and spend each day wisely. Working from their sense of purpose, they seek to set a personal mission that will allow them to plant, nurture and grow the best possible life.

Quaker theologian Elton Trueblood wrote, "We have made at least a start in discovering the meaning in human life when we plant shade trees under which we know full well we will never sit." Planting trees whose shade we may never enjoy is an acknowledgment and commitment that we will use our lives to the fullest. Using all your energies and talents to plant what you know full well you may never harvest is a profound tribute to your life, personhood and existence.

• For what are you saving your energies, your abilities or your life? What will you gain by banking your life for a rainy day?

• What are you willing to give your time, talents and treasures to, even though you may never see your dream become a reality in your lifetime?

What Will Be Your Contribution?

You are not here merely to make a living. You are here in order to enable the world to live more amply, with greater vision, with a finer spirit of hope and achievement. You are here to enrich the world, and you impoverish yourself if you forget the errand.

—Woodrow Wilson
28th President of the United States
(1856-1924)

AT TIMES, LIFE BECOMES A BLUR. Hours turn into days, rolling into weeks, and are quietly multiplied into years. The necessity of earning a living compounds the time exponentially, and before too long, you are in the waning days of your life, perplexed that you have not accomplished your dreams.

Leaders realize—in the timeline of eternity—that they are on this blue ball for a blink of an eye. Acknowledging that fact, they contemplate what enrichment they should bring while alive. Leaders toil to understand their personal mission and purpose amid the variety of tasks pressing them for atten-

19

tion. With courage, effective leaders place the writing of a personal mission as a priority to all these other obligations. For without personal mission, leaders realize they may reach the end of life having made a good living, only to know they are impoverished for a lack of purpose in the striving.

- At the end of your life looking back, what will make you happy and give you a feeling that what you have done is worthwhile? What have you done that will live beyond your own existence?
- Can you think across your life and have no regrets?
- What do you desire to have said about you at your own funeral by your family, friends and the community in which you live?
- Is your mission in life centered on universal principles, such as integrity, service and love?

Avoid Self-Absorption

Try to care about something in this vast world besides the gratification of small selfish desires. Try to care for what is best in thought and action—something that is good apart from the accidents of your own lot. Look on other lives besides your own. See what their troubles are, and how they are borne.

—George Eliot
English novelist
(1819-1880)

IT IS EASY IN LIFE to become self-absorbed. Misfortune, busyness, or even a string of good days can turn your attention from those around you to total introspection. This self-focus may monopolize your time. Self-focus can rob you of the joy of living. There is always danger in spending huge amounts of time preparing to overcome roadblocks or working to insure there will be more days of prosperity instead of really living.

Our children were funny to watch when they were little, particularly when it came to playing make believe. Sarah and David spent a great deal of time preparing for their fun. It was not unusual for Sarah to work diligently for an hour getting everything ready, while her brother dutifully assisted. What made the activity amusing was as they completed their work in setting up the scenario, they discontinued playing! They were so self focused in preparation that they never spent any time actually having fun.

Living fully means you must focus on something beyond yourself, being careful not to spend all your time preparing and readying to live. Leaders acknowledge there is a balance between self-prosperity, preparation and leaving a legacy. Sole focus on any of these may bring imbalance to life. Yet if there is an imbalance, leaders err on the side of leaving this world with a legacy that creates the "best in thought and action" for those that follow.

- In your retirement years, what will make you smile?
- What are you willing to commit yourself to and act upon at this moment in your life that will give you satisfaction and some legacy for the future?
- What do you believe God has called you to be, do or undertake with your life?

Go the Distance

*It is always important to have something
yet to do in life.*

—Victor Frankl
concentration camp survivor;
Viennese-born psychiatrist
1905-1997)

A PLAGUE OF MODERN AMERICAN CULTURE is the
concept of retirement. Annually, thousands of citizens reach
an age of retirement only to find they may have 15 to 20
years of life left to enjoy or despise. The chilling fact is that
these "golden years" represent nearly ½ of their previous
active working careers. The question is, "What will you do
with these years? Will the final two decades of your life be
boring or soaring?"

Jimmy and Rosalyn Carter write in their book, *Everything
to Gain: Making the Most of the Rest of Your Life*, about the
weeks and months following their Presidential defeat and
return to Plains, Georgia. Immediately they began busying
themselves with setting up their new lives, reconnecting with
their roots and planning for the Presidential Library.

As the library plans and architectural designs began to
take shape, Rosalyn and Jimmy felt empty about its future

and impact on the world. Rosalyn recalls that after one meeting, Jimmy declared there would be no Carter Library.

One night, Rosalyn woke up startled to find Jimmy sitting in the darkness on their bed. He shared at that moment his dream for a place where nations could come together privately to resolve their differences. Believing it a place of conflict resolution, Carter envisioned a center founded on peace. It was to be a place where nations could privately negotiate their problems without publicity, fanfare or possible political embarrassment. It would be a center designed for settling disputes. So in the middle of a still Georgia night, the Carter Presidential Center was born. This now one-term, ex-US President became bent on peaceful resolve to critical issues of the world for the rest of his life.

Leaders bent on living a full life—to the very end—know what they will undertake in their "new careers." They have clarified and set goals for the years after receiving the "gold watch." These people have calculated and prepared for how they will spend life while still in their 30s, 40s and 50s. Leaders focused on a full life adhere to the motto, "Don't die until you are dead."

• Are you fulfilling your meaning of life through your current work assignment? Why or why not? (Posed by Victor Frankl.)

• Are you contributing to the quality of human life by helping others realize their special purpose through your current work position? Why or why not? (Posed by Victor Frankl.)

• What are your plans for the "golden years"? Are they boring or soaring? Are they focused on productivity or inactivity? List out your hoped for "retirement" plans and the dreams you have for these years.

Dare to Dream

All men dream, but not equally. Those men who dream by night in the dusty recesses of their minds wake in the morning to find it was but vanity, but those men who dream by day—these are dangerous men, for they dream with open eyes to make their dreams come true.

—T. E. Lawrence
British soldier
(1888-1935)

WE ARE CREATURES OF FANTASY. We enjoy make believe, wishful thinking and living vicariously through the "rich and famous." Dreaming of what could or should be is an alluring diversion from the daily routine.

Fantasy is healthy and an exercise for our imagination. Yet building castles in the air can be debilitating, leading to inactivity if we spend all our time wishing these fortresses were our residences.

Daydreaming—coupled with action and persistence—can be world changing. Skeptical men saw Orville and Wilbur Wright as fanciful dreamers. Their flight on December 17, 1903, was so non-newsworthy that only four newspapers inaccurately reported the Kitty Hawk event, and their hometown paper did not mention the flight. Even the U.S. government did not take their offer of airplane usage seriously, although they had several successful flights in 1905. But these brothers were dangerous men, dreaming with eyes open. Their belief in the possibility of flight has transformed the world as maybe no other invention of the modern era.

Their dreaming, shaped by action and risk, sent them "flying through the clouds of the impossible." Your dreaming and risk taking may be as influential on the world as that of the Wright Brothers. Dream in the light of day and see what you can make happen during your lifetime.

• What are your dreams for your career? Your relationships? Your civic service?

• Why do you want to make these dreams realities?

• Will you become the person your mission articulates if you achieve these dreams? How will this happen?

Believe in
Your Dreams

If you can dream it, you can do it.
Always remember this whole thing started
with a mouse.

—Walt Disney
animator & motion picture producer
(1901-1966)

HE COULD HARDLY PAY the family bills. The garage, which was his workshop, contained equipment that had cost his life savings. Yet the dream that he could "do it" fixed his imagination and provided the light in the darkness of that makeshift office.

The Mouse emerging from the garage began humbly. But that happy rodent blazed the trail for modern motion pictures and animation. A listing of Disney's achievements hallmarks what the inspiration of a Mouse spurred:

1928—The Mickey Mouse cartoon shown with sound and color

1932—The film, *Flowers and Trees,* is the first in Technicolor

1937—The first full-length cartoon film, *Snow White*

1950—Disney sees the opportunity of TV (which others disregarded) and pilots a weekly program, *The Wonderful World of Disney*

1953—The first full-length film with animals in the wild, *The Living Desert*

1955—The opening of Disneyland Park

Over forty-five Academy Awards for films, scientific and technological advances in the motion picture industry

If a mouse fashioned from vision, goals and optimism can impact the world, what could your dreams set in motion?

- Which of your dreams could become realities if you were willing to put in the necessary effort? Be specific.
- If you spent time thinking through your dreams, what are the specific goals needed to convert your dreams into reality?
- List the goals from the question above by priority. Rank these goals beginning with the number one. In the margin next to these goals, write the date you will begin to work on this goal.

Your Life's Legacy: Chance or Choice?

Destiny is not a matter of chance, it is a matter of choice.

—William Jennings Bryan
U.S. Secretary of State
(1860-1925)

HAVE YOU EVER READ THE ODDS of winning a sweepstakes? They are astronomical—one in millions of chances. Yet millions of people base their destinies on a chance rather than daily working to make their "dreams come true."

Just as winning millions in a sweepstakes is a chance, so is your life outcome if it is based on accepting whatever happens to you each day. Missions and goals become reality only by choice—a daily choice. The ultimate question is, "Will you choose chance or choice?" With chance, fate is the major factor. With choice, you are the designer and contributor to your future.

• Are you currently living your life by chance? Are you living at the decisions of others?

• What choices will you have to make in life if you are to overcome what fate may deliver to you in your old age?

• What goals do you need to write down and work toward if you are to be the architect of your life?

Narrowing
Your Focus

He who doubts is like a wave of the sea,
blown and tossed by the wind.

—The Apostle James
The Bible, James 1:6

BUSINESS **MANAGEMENT DECISION-MAKERS** call
it opportunity cost. You and I call it choosing between 'this
or that.' In developing and writing a personal mission, you
will be forced to make decisions between many good alter-
natives. In considering your life purpose, you will be challenged to focus on those opportunities that will produce the
results you desire to achieve. If you are to make your mission
a reality, you must be willing to prune away what might be
enticing and worthwhile for what is critical and essential to
you as a human being.

Life continually presents you with a variety of worthwhile and noble causes. But if you are not careful in sifting
out what leads you to fulfilling your mission, the siren's song
of alternative opportunities will cause you to doubt your current path. Ultimately, you may be frustrated by your journey
if you begin to move back and forth between what is right to
do and what is fun.

Your mission will determine your opportunity costs. If you have ever felt overwhelmed by the number of requests for your time, talents and energies, consider laying the invitations to boards, community programs and donor requests against the gauge of your mission. While many of the requests you receive may be noble, keeping your mission in focus will help you make the appropriate decisions without becoming sidetracked.

James the Apostle warns you to consider the multitude of opportunities before you, keeping in mind to choose with confidence what is right for your mission. Without willingness or courage to choose what is needed to achieve your life purpose, you will be unsettled, driven by the expedient, not the long term.

• What are the current programs, activities or commitments in your life that are keeping you from making your mission a reality?

• Do you allow so many activities and requests from others to invade your life that you are now sidetracked from achieving your life purpose?

Dismantle the Quick-Fix Myth

*In most things success depends on
knowing how long it takes to succeed.*

—Charles Louis de Montesquieu
French philosopher
(1689-1755)

WE ARE ENTHRALLED WITH INSTANT SUCCESS.
Fast weight loss programs, scratch-off lottery fortunes and
30-days-to-a-better-you headline hundreds of voices that tell
us success is a day away.

It is unfortunate that when we look at successful people,
we either forget or never consider that they spent long hours
or years working at their dreams. A crucial ingredient to all
success is calculating the time needed to convert goals into
accomplishments. Without figuring the cost, you may easily
become sidetracked or loose heart for reaching success, especially when you are under pressure or there are many days
without a glimmer of achievement.

Taped to my computer monitor is a magazine clipping. It
is a short list, but one important reminder that success comes
only by persistence and hard work. The short list describes
the amount of time some noted authors spent working on

their book manuscripts before they were accepted by a publisher. A few authors listed are John Grisham, whose work, *A Time to Kill*, was rejected twenty-eight times; William Golding, whose *Lord of the Flies*, was rejected twenty-one times, and Pearl Buck whose classic, *The Good Earth*, was turned away fourteen times. Yet they were determined to achieve their dreams, and by submitting their manuscripts one more time, they found success waiting.

Determining the ratio of time to goal attainment may be the most basic element to fulfilling your mission. Without calculating this ratio, you may not only lose the battle, but the war.

• How long will it take you to reach your desired goals and hoped for purposes?

• Are you willing to plant and tend your goals over the long term to achieve them? Are you willing to face failure and barriers in the immediate to achieve the best at the end of your life?

Be Prepared

To be prepared is half the victory.

—Miguel de Cervantes
author of *Don Quixote*
(1547-1616)

As **A TEACHER, I OFTEN WITNESS** the dire stress of students as the next test approaches. When the exam is handed out, many quickly leaf through the pages with a heavy sigh. In grading these tests, I also realize those that sigh the loudest often illustrate their lack of preparation in their responses. With a few hours of study, these students may have easily won the day.

It seems such simple advice. Yet being prepared is the hardest for us to incorporate. Being prepared is not a motto only for young scouts, but for everyone set on achieving their dreams. Half of the victory is preparation. The other half is using those tools necessary for the task at hand. Preparation coupled with proactivity is a sure victory.

There are people who believe that many of the successes found in life are a matter of luck. But the noted researcher of peak performers, Charles Garfield, discovered that successful people make their own luck. They make their own luck by preparing for the future and making choices now that will reap rewards later. Success is a matter of being prepared in advance for what lies ahead. Then at the point you reach your life dreams, it will be accomplishment through preparation and proactivity, not luck.

• What preparation do you need to undertake that will make reaching your dreams easier? For example, do you need a college degree, venture capital or a speech course? Make a list of areas/skills/knowledge you will need to expand if you are to be successful. Next to these items, note when you will start and how you will achieve success through this preparation.
• Are you willing to make the necessary choices now so that when the opportunities come, your dreams will be fulfilled?

Share Your Vision

Use every letter you write, every conversation you have to express your beliefs and dreams; affirm to others your vision of the world.

—Robert Miller
former U.N. Assistant Secretary
General of the United States

CREATING A PERSONAL MISSION statement, establishing goals and advancing toward fulfillment of your dreams can become self-focused. It is almost certain that if you spend considerable time reflecting and working alone on these statements, you will become isolated from others.

Yet if you are to be transformed, as well as to influence the world around you, you must own and articulate those ideals. Communicating your mission through words and actions not only keeps the flame alive in you, but it also contains the power to ignite a passion and calling in others.

On the back of my business card is my personal mission statement. I place it there for others that I might do business with, either now or in the future. My mission statement is there as the framework for my relationship with them. It is the beginning point of all we will share and undertake together—at least from my side of the venture.

But the mission statement is also there for me. I apply this mission statement to my business card with a self-adhesive label. This label is raised enough off the back of the card to be noticeable. Now it may sound funny, but every time I hand out that mission statement, my fingers rub against it and I find myself recommitting to my life purpose once again. A small label on an announcement of my business is a constant affirmation of my hopes for the future.

It may seem a small oversight not to share your personal mission and goals, but in reality, it has profound implications for yourself and others.

• Sharing your mission with others gives you public ownership of those beliefs. How might you find ways to share your personal mission with others?

• Consider using the back of your business card as an announcement of your mission and dreams.

Accomplishment=
Vision + Action

*A burning purpose attracts others who
are drawn along with it and help fulfill it.*

—Margaret Bourke-White
American photographer & writer;
1st female war correspondent WWII
(1906-1971)

A STORY TOLD ABOUT GENERAL EISENHOWER and
a piece of string is fitting for thinking about your mission,
purpose and life goals. It seems before a major battle of
WWII, General Eisenhower was in a strategy briefing with
his commanders. Knowing that many men could lose their
lives this day, Eisenhower stood before the assembly and laid
a piece of string on the table in front of him. Looking at the
soldiers, he began to push the string, which immediately
balled up. Eisenhower said, "When you push people to do
something, while you stand by barking, they cannot see the
bigger picture. They become resistant to the demands of the
occasion and suffer defeat." Then Eisenhower took the same
string and pulled it across the table. The string, becoming
straight and moving with ease, advanced from one side to
the other. At this Eisenhower remarked, "But if your mission

is clear, passionate and full of purpose for a larger good, people will rise to the occasion and victory will be assured."

For several years, I have conducted a non-scientific but accurate study concerning mission and passion. This study revolves around two questions. I first ask people what they do in their daily work assignment. Most dutifully explain their career or jobs, but not always with enthusiasm.

After I receive an explanation for the first question, I ask people to tell me their avocations, life hobbies or personal mission. With this question comes enthusiasm and passion that oozes with every word and beams from their eyes. Inevitably, they tell me how people come into their lives, giving them needed encouragement or assistance with their dreams. While most have only begun and others are close to achieving their goals, they all express how their passion draws others to them, like pulling a string.

Your personal mission, purpose and goals will pull others to them when they are bigger than yourself. And when you couple this larger picture of the world with your passion for the cause, people will help you fulfill your dreams—to the very last victory.

• While you may have dreams and specific goals for your leadership and your personal future, are you passionate about their fulfillment? Why or why not?

• If these dreams and goals do not inspire passion in you, what will it take to make them more inspirational to you and others?

Radiate Passion

*I am convinced that my life belongs to
the whole community; and as long as I live,
it is my privilege to do for it whatever I can,
for the harder I work the more I live. I
rejoice in life for its own sake. Life is no brief
candle to me. It is a sort of splendid torch
which I got hold of for a moment, and I want
to make it burn as brightly as possible before
turning it over to future generations.*

—George Bernard Shaw
Irish-born playwright
(1856-1950)

KEVIN, **A MEMBER OF MY COMMUNITY,** caught my
attention and my ear as I stood in a fast food line, while he
was perched at a nearby table with his family. "Our staff met
today for five hours about our ministry's mission. And you
know what?" he said with a confident voice and the light of
enthusiasm gleaming from his eyes. "We have never wavered
from that mission since our founding!" Kevin's presence and
passion for his ministry were commanding. While others
looked at Kevin with blank stares, I could not help being
attracted to his enthusiasm.

I reflected on Kevin's passion for his ministry to homeless persons and substance addicted individuals over the next few days. I recalled another encounter with Kevin at a gas station late on a Friday evening. It was there that Kevin was engaging the attendant in a passionate conversation about helping others and serving those in need of dignity and hope. What a profound effect Kevin has had on the lives of forgotten scores of citizens in my community. What passion is alive in this once successful real estate agent now turned evangelist.

Your life purpose, like Kevin's, should not only draw you to action, but should create a longing of your mind, body and spirit to undertake what is necessary to produce good work. On those occasions of indecision and insecurity, this heart desire should dare you to act, over and over, with an undaunted determination and passion.

I serve on a community leadership board with Kevin. What joy, challenge, confrontation and idealism he brings to that organization. Whether it is a discussion of youth, the training of adults or the image of the organization, Kevin is sure to share with passionate animation his faith, his belief in people and his hope for the best possible world for all God's creatures. While people may shrink from Kevin's intensity at times, there is no disguising the purpose or passion that drives his every waking moment. We would all do well to be so engaged in our own life's calling.

• Do you long to make your life purpose a reality? In the quiet moments of your life, do you ache to live your mission to its fullest?

• Are you willing to share publicly your mission and motivation with others, even if all eyes would be on you in wonder?

Live with Courage

Saying is one thing doing is another.

—Michel Eyquem de Montainge
French essayist
(1533-1592)

SUCCESSFUL LEADERS KNOW it is one thing to have a mission statement about the values and purposes they believe and quite another thing to live by those ideals. Living out your mission is a choice to internalize the principles and values of that statement while daring to live them out daily. Allowing your mission to guide you even in the darkest moments of life is about choice and obedience to universally correct principles.

I have personally experienced first hand the excellence and commitment a mission extracts from us, if we are willing to live according to our intended outcomes. At a time of deep pain in my personal life, with both family and friends, I was at the point of throwing in the proverbial towel. At the age of fifteen, my daughter shared with my wife and me that she was pregnant. In tremendous sorrow and disparaging grief, our family was confronted with social stigma, the pain of failure and the stress of broken relationships. There seemed no escape from the anguish of our family, with relationships of decades about to collapse into a heap of despair.

I personally agonized over my role and public image as a parent, business professional and community leader. I was literally drowning in the advice and counsel of others that provided remedies in this most transforming circumstance. The counsel and advice was often helpful. Yet through it all, the counsel of others was beckoning me to make a choice between my pride, status and image or my family, self-respect and spiritual wholeness. I was lost.

But on a hot July day in a Washington DC hotel room, I took my written mission statement from my planner and began reading it again. I read it over and over, reflecting on my life, faith, what I wanted to count for and what I had committed to be and do, both personally and professionally. I realized the ensuing decisions and emotions were not easy to face nor was there a quick-fix solution. Staying true to my mission gave me a renewed strength and confidence that a win/win could be realized in this painful life moment. My commitment to mission made me become a problem solver, not one who abdicates in time of crisis. In reflection, I have come to realize that abandoning my mission in the face of great adversity would have diminished me as a human being. This abandonment would have been a far greater loss than the enormous and gut wrenching decisions about status or image. Staying true to my faith and mission provided a way to reconcile with my daughter and work together for a life that has since brought health, happiness, love and peace to everyone, including my granddaughter.

Developing a mission, writing it down and committing yourself to the action steps it may call you to undertake provide a place for you to stand in today's harried and unsettling world. As a leader, you must be willing to drive in the stake of values and principles, while not moving from what is important to yourself, your family or your organization, no matter the call of popular opinion. In the face of adversity and challenge, living a life consistent with your mission produces excellence and a life that will not be compromised.

• Are there ideals, values or principles that will call you to a specific course of action if confronted to choose your mission over public opinion?

• Do you have the courage to allow your mission to guide you through the difficult issues you might face in life?

Act True to
Your Mission

*Woe to you, for you are like
whitewashed tombs, which outwardly
appear beautiful, but within they are full of
dead men's bones. . . . So you also
outwardly appear righteous to men, but
within you are full of hypocrisy and iniquity.*

—Jesus the Christ
The Bible, Matthew 23:27

THE HEADLINE SHOCKED YOU like an icy cold shower
on a sleepy morning. A prominent and publicly lauded CEO
was released for moral and legal improprieties. Over the
course of several days, a CEO of influence and public esteem
was reduced to discussion in hushed conversations. How
could it happen?

There is an awful tendency to contemplate a mission
statement, write down the words and proclaim it is finished!
It is easy to believe that the words alone carry some magical
power that if mouthed occasionally will protect us from the
results of our most wayward decisions. Mission statements
are only a picture of our desired future. It is the willingness

to take our pulse of actions against those words that determine our course, balance and direction.

It is essential for the leader to keep the mission in focus at all times. A written mission statement is no more than platitudes or a novel idea if it is not reviewed constantly with the intention to check one's actions and life against its principles. If leaders are serious about fulfilling either their organizational or personal missions, they will deliberately ask questions regarding course correction regularly.

The Gospel of Matthew records this pronouncement of Jesus about graves and whitewashed tombs. Jesus criticizes those who outwardly profess to be living rightly—a whitewashed tomb—only to open their mouths and reveal the rotting contents of the grave. Leaders, or for that matter anyone, can write and publicly recite a mission statement. But the leader who is followed will be the one that speaks it, lives it and privately checks his or her intentions against its principles and expectations on a regular basis.

- Are you living inwardly and outwardly in a manner consistent with your mission?
- Are your intentions, secret desires, private ambitions, dreams or passions contradictory to what you publicly proclaim about yourself or your organization?
- Are the decisions you make congruent with the principles of your mission?

Don't Delay
Living Healthily

May you live all the days of your life.

—Jonathan Swift
English author
(1667-1745)

"IT IS A TRAGEDY THAT PEOPLE ARE DYING eight hours every day." Morris Massey, author and professional speaker, caught the audience with that simple statement. Traveling the globe, Massey has encountered people of all races working in a "zombie" state of life. The true tragedy is that they may "die with their song still inside them."

Living all the days of your life means doing what is necessary NOW. It means continually stoking the fires of dreams as you attempt to make them real. It also means not putting off till tomorrow what you can do today. Whether we intend to our not, we are creatures of habit, eventually living out the words of St. Augustine, "By and By never comes."

You may consider it unusual to find narrative about health in a section on mission. But in the last few years, I have come to realize that if I am unhealthy, I may physically never complete my mission or worse, may die before I have had the chance to live. Yet our view on health is again like

47

that of St. Augustine's insight, we plan to be healthy, but by and by never comes.

My wife is the health advocate in our family. Following her certification of aerobics from the Cooper Institute, she dove deeply into ten years of instructing others in fitness. But her enthusiasm for health only sank in for me in that last few years. While she labored vigorously to remain healthy, I kept putting off exercise for a time when it would be conducive to my schedule. But by and by never comes.

It wasn't until writing this book that I came to realize I will never complete my personal dreams or life mission unless I am physically healthy. So with determination, I began to watch my weight, eat all things in moderation and began exercising. Through this newfound insight, I now realize that maintaining unhealthy lifestyles is a choice of self gratification above fulfilling your life mission or sharing the possibility of wonderful relationships all the days of your life. Maintaining a lifestyle balanced in eating, exercising and keeping up your spiritual and mental well being are essential to completing your purpose for being here.

It is necessary for us to actively live every moment and day of our lives so that LODI does not set in, that is, "The Law of Diminishing Intent." The further away you travel from your mission, goals and action steps, the more likely it is you will never complete what is dear to your heart. Carpe Diem!

• What have you done this week to further your mission or goals? Make a list.

• Review your goals from previous weeks. What three (3) goals or actions steps did you write that you have yet to undertake? Write them below, noting the day this week you will begin.

• What unhealthy aspects of your lifestyle do you continue to entertain that will keep you from living a full life? What commitments will you make today to start living in greater health? Are there unhealthy habits you must overcome to live all the days of your life?

Rage Like a River

Our nature lies in movement; complete rest is death.

—Blaise Pascal
French philosopher (*Pensées*)
(1623-1662)

THE **DIFFERENCE IS ASTOUNDING.** Consider the appearance of a swamp. It is a motionless mass of water, often a stagnant place inhospitable for most living things. While there is a delicate ecosystem that thrives in these places, it is not one much suited for humans.

But a river, what a difference. Flowing, moving, purifying itself as it cascades over rocks and pebbles. It is also a source of power as it bursts through turbines created to capture its energy. A river can bring life, refreshment and recreation to the environment surrounding it.

It is our human nature to need movement. Our dreams and goals, if clear and passionate, will pull us forward to their completion. The sadness of humanity is that while many people are walking around, breathing and moving, they are already dead—lifeless from lack of direction, purpose, and meaning. The challenge is to keep your flame burning brightly all the days of your life.

- On a scale of 1-10, how passionate do you feel about your life goals and dreams? Why?
- Do you feel more alive since beginning your reading and answering questions? Why or why not?
- What actions do you need to set in motion that will add zeal to your dreams, goals and life?

Find Joy in Your Efforts

Far and away the best prize that life offers is the chance to work hard at work worth doing.

—Theodore Roosevelt
Labor Day Speech, 1903
26th President of United States
(1858-1919)

I HAVE HEARD PEOPLE throughout my life share their chosen profession as "a labor of love." It is noticeable that these persons share their remarks with passion, spark and enthusiasm for completing work they believe promotes a common good for all people. While many of these persons work in careers they "love," others also share a similar exhilaration for their life mission and purpose.

Before the Apostle Paul was put to death by the ancient Roman government, he wrote, "I have run the race and fought the good fight for the prize of the high calling of God." Working hard for the worthy prize of a fulfilled life, a transformed self, a better family, job or community is our highest calling. While it may or may not reap fame or fortune, it will present the victory crown for a life lived well.

Over the Winter Season of leadership and personal development, you have been challenged to create a mission statement, set specific goals and risk for their fulfillment. How are you doing at this point in the journey? What have you accomplished and what remains to be done? Make a list of these in the columns below:

GOALS I SET AND AM ACHIEVING

_____

_____

_____

_____

_____

_____

_____

_____

_____

_____

GOALS THAT ARE AHEAD

_____

_____

_____

_____

_____

_____

_____

_____

_____

_____

Does Your Work Fit with Your Mission?

Most people spend most of their days doing what they do not want to do in order to earn the right, at times, to do what they may desire.

—John Mason Brown
American drama critic & biographer
(1900-1969)

SPENDING ONE'S LIFE WORKING AT TASKS that are not fulfilling or contrary to our dreams is tragic. Yet many work day in and day out in the hope that they will at some point have the opportunity to pursue their life ambitions. The problem is that all too soon, life is over and those yearnings for something different go with us to the grave. Unaware, people become unequally yoked to vocations that keep them earthbound instead of setting them free to live their life purposes.

There are times in our lives when change must come and we must make decisions about those unrealized dreams. Your energies, time and dreams are sapped when you remain yoked to circumstances that are not right for you. While it takes heart to make changes, mustering the fortitude to break free is critical if you are to succeed in living your personal mission or life calling.

How can you survive if you are unequally yoked in spirit, attitude, ethical stance, work ethic or principled lifestyle to your current work obligations? A poorly fitted yoke on a beast of burden creates pressure against the animals neck, choking it. What a dismal metaphor for life when the pressure of unequal yoking chokes out your hopes, dreams and passions. Being mismatched with your current work situation is a difficult reality to accept. Yet being aware of that condition may free you to consider other opportunities that will help you achieve your potential.

In an age of complexity there is simplicity, if you are courageous enough to step away from the calling of the crowd to the calling of your purpose.

• Do you feel choked by your current working environment for any reasons, be they ethical, moral, or principled?

• Do you have a calling that you continue to discount? What would it take for you to begin planning to move toward your life calling?

• Have you spent time setting goals to obtain your life calling? How might these goals be realized? Who can help you make your goals obtainable? Are you willing to risk—even in small ways—to begin moving toward your life dreams and mission?

Evaluate Your Commitment

*The kingdom of heaven is like a mustard
seed, which a man took and planted in his field.
Though it is the smallest of all your seeds, yet
when it grows, it is the largest of garden plants
and becomes a tree, so that the birds of the air
come and perch in its branches.*

—Jesus the Christ
The Bible, Matthew 13:31

SEEDS ARE CONTAINERS OF TRANSFORMATION.
All over the earth, hundreds of thousands of seeds provide
the capsule for nature's life forms to germinate, grow and
bear fruit. The tiniest of seeds contains the power to become
towering redwoods, great whales that roam the sea, and
human life.

Just as seeds provide the beginning of life, the seeds of
ideas, planted in a receptive mind, begin a transformation of
the individual. The development of your personal mission
and recognition of your life purpose is a seed that, once
planted, begins to mature and grow to full bloom. As the
seed of personal mission takes root, it changes you. It is
interesting, too, that these seeds of personal mission will not

only change you but will summon others to plant seeds of purpose in their lives as well. As a ripple in still water produces circle upon circle, the seeds of personal mission produce enough power to recreate—little by little—our entire society. Amazing dimensions of transformation occur from the planting of small seeds.

Your challenge is to plant your mission deep in your heart. Planting your mission allows its power to germinate and bear fruit. If you can spare a few minutes every day to nurture your personal mission and life purpose, your life will begin to take shape and grow to full bloom in ways you may never have considered before.

There are opportunities for leadership all around us. While you may not become a CEO or even a legendary leader, the development of your mission will bring your best efforts to the surface. So whether you are an hourly employee, a supervisor, a CEO, a student or unemployed, working at understanding your life mission is a task that will bear fruit throughout your lifetime.

In the end, your personal mission will bear fruit as a result of all your planting, cultivating, nurturing and tending. The astonishing fact about fruit is that it, too, contains new seeds that will produce more fruit. Ultimately, the fully grown life purpose must be planted in others so that they may be challenged to grow into what they were created to be.

The mustard seed is a small seed. Yet when fully grown, it is one of the largest shrubs. Your personal mission is like this small seed. You must take personal responsibility for watering, tending and nurturing your mission if it is to become healthy and strong. Without tending carefully to your mission, it is vulnerable to being uprooted, burned out or trampled by the problems, crises, and busyness of daily life.

Planting, growing and harvesting is an investment of time, energy, and commitment. Simply planting will not ensure a harvest or yield bounteous crops. Leaders take the time daily to practice and safeguard the young seedling of purpose taking root in them. When all is said and done, there can be no reaping of character or effective leadership without intentionally planting, tending and nurturing your mission.

- Are you really committed to spending the necessary time in developing and living out your mission?
- Are you willing to risk, challenge or redirect your life in ways that will reflect your mission, while making it healthy and strong?
- Do you believe your mission will bear fruit? In what ways?

Spice up Your Life

Our real freedom comes from being aware
that we do not have to save the world, merely
make a difference in the place where we live.

—Parker Palmer
philosopher and author

AROMAS CAPTURE US. Advertising agencies know well that pitching the aroma of perfume, scented sprays in aerosol cans and the joy of waking up to fresh brewed coffee excites the senses more than a photograph. Aromas can also stimulate our memories of experiences, pleasures or places we have visited in the past. The enjoyment of life is contained in the scents around us, whether it's an unfolding flower, a kitchen full of savory cooking or a synthetic potion.

Both personal and organizational missions add a fragrance to life. A clearly articulated mission not only directs your thoughts and movements, but it also lends a gusto, aroma or flavor to your journey. As early as 380 BC, Aristotle summoned humankind to reflect on their existence and then consider what it means to live well. In our own time, the psychiatrist Victor Frankl reminds us that "the striving to find one's meaning in life is the primary motivational force of humankind." You add fragrance to your life through reflection and consideration of your existence, as well as in tending the seeds of purpose you plant in your life as a leader and human being. Additionally, you intensify the pungent scent of life when you capture your reflections in a personal mission that calls you to your best efforts.

A personal mission aids you in locating your place of purpose in the world. Mission conveys a clarity about yourself, while helping you to focus your energies during this earthly journey. It is a fallacy to believe that goal setting alone will fulfill your deepest desires for direction and purpose. By planting seeds of abundant living formulated in a personal mission statement, you add fragrance to your goals, aroma to your path.

Freedom and abundant living come to you through the culmination of reflecting on, writing, reinforcing and working intensely on a personal mission. Planted within a mission is a course of action, as well as opportunities for choice. These choices, however, are more than simply deciding "should I work on this project or that one" or "be involved with this program or another." The real freedom, as Palmer observes, comes from the awareness you do not have to save the world, but you do need to make a difference where you are planted.

There is around every human being a "scent circle." Within this arm's length circle are aromas of the human body, whether naturally distilled or applied with cosmetics. People around you are welcomed or repelled, depending on your fragrance. A mission built on universal principles creates an aroma that will draw people into your circle, a sphere of influence where you can make a difference. The by-product of this close personal interaction is a challenge for others to create their own wonderful fragrance. You have a choice of the scent you apply by extracting it from the seeds you consciously plant. The fragrance of your personal mission can be captivating, inviting and liberating, not only for your own spirit, but for the lives of those within your reach.

• What aroma do you give off to those around you? Is your life purpose inviting or repelling?

• Through the focus of your mission, do you feel free of the need to save the entire planet?

Writing a Personal
Mission Statement

DURING THIS TIME OF READING in the Winter Season, you have been reflecting about your life and your future dreams. It is time to consider placing these thoughts into a written mission statement.

Personal mission statements are a central part of the effective leader and person's life. Out of the mission grow the goals and actions that set the pace and accomplishment of one's life hopes.

To begin the mission writing process, follow the steps below. These steps assist you in creating and writing your personal mission statement. The remainder of this book will help make that mission a reality.

STEP ONE:

From the responses you have considered as you read the Winter Season, list out the ideals, values and character traits that are of greatest importance to you. They may be core values like, love, wisdom, care, integrity, truthfulness, legacy, morality, encouragement, happiness, friendship, fame, justice, joy, family and so on.

Taking the list, arrange these values into an order of priority—1 through 10. Consider this list again and reduce it to three core values that you could not live without upholding or pursuing. If you would be diminished as a person if any of the three would be taken away, these are probably the core values for you.

STEP TWO:

Try writing a sample mission statement from this list of core values. This statement will help guide you and keep you focused on your preferred future. The statement should be action oriented, such as, "It is my desire to be a loving, caring and compassionate person." The statement should be a challenge to you and something you are passionate about. It should also require courage and risk taking from you if the statement is to become a reality.

Laurie Beth Jones, author of *Jesus, CEO,* suggests three elements to writing this mission statement and keeping it focused. They are: 1) your mission statement should be only one sentence, 2) it should be simple enough for a twelve-year-old to understand and recite, and 3) you can recite this statement at "gun point," remembering that time is of the essence in achieving your life mission.

Allow me to share my personal mission statement. It was originally written in 1989 but has become clearer over the past decade. While the original thought and intent of the mission statement have not changed, the words have become clearer and more defining. Your challenge will be to review your mission statement regularly, updating it and finding more accurate ways to describe what you want to achieve in life. My personal mission is: inviting people to an abundant life by choosing God's best.

STEP THREE:

Commitment to your mission is important if it is to be realized. A deep sense of commitment to your mission will sustain you in times of stress, difficulty and dire uncertainty. Complete the following statement and keep it handy for review.

"I am committed to my personal mission because . . ."

I also challenge you to share your mission with the confidant in your life. Ask them to keep you accountable to your mission and life purpose. Utilize their relationship to help you stay focused, committed and action oriented in reaching your dreams.

The mission you are building must:
- Create meaning for your life
- Set a standard of excellence that stretches you
- Bridge your present with your preferred future
- Transcend the status quo
- Attract both your commitment & your energy

GOAL SETTING AND ACTION STEPS FOR MAKING YOUR MISSION A REALITY

Words and missions without actions just pass the time and make us feel good. Setting goals, with time frames, makes those purposes become realities. It is sad to consider that in our Western Culture, only 1% of people have any written goals. Most people spend their time wishing their lives and circumstances would be different. But "wishing" without goals and action will continue to give a person what they have always had in the past. Goals and action are the ingredients that move us toward success.

The first step for setting goals and moving forward is deciding you will do it. H.L. Hunt stated, "For things to change, you must decide to change." Without that commitment, your goals, no matter how noble, will never be accomplished. Additionally, you must decide exactly what you want, determine the price you must pay to get what you desire, and continue to pay that price until you have fulfilled your dreams.

With these remarks shared, it is time to write some goals. From your personal mission, write three goals that will help you accomplish what you desire in life. These goals should be specific, not just general statements. They must also list the reason for wanting to achieve them. Use my example for writing your goal and steps to achieve it:

"It is my goal to write and publish 100 articles in magazines, newsletters and periodicals. They are in the categories of leadership, customer service, personal mission and life legacy. I am writing these articles to stay intellectually fresh, enhance my writing and communication skills, to develop an expertise in these four fields and to invite people to think about their futures and lives in an abundant way. Writing and publishing five articles a year keeps me moving toward 100 articles."

As you can see, this goal is specific, providing a reason for the writing and how I know I am working on the goal—five articles a year. You must be this specific, so that your goals have a reason and an evaluation tool embedded within their framework.

Once you have written the goal, set a beginning date and a check date for the goal. Write these dates next to each goal. I review my goals monthly, with a major check point at the beginning of every year. This continually keeps me focused on whether I am achieving the goals that will help me fulfill my life mission.

I recommend starting with three or four goals related to your mission. If you write too many goals, you may become overwhelmed. Keep your goals and objectives manageable in order to move steadily toward fulfilling your mission and avoiding burnout or dismay.

Remember that having a mission statement is a powerful tool! But the tool is only as good as your commitment and willingness to make your preferred future a reality. From this point forward, realizing your purpose will take commitment, personal energy, action and continual reflection for course corrections. For more information on goal setting, listen to the audio tape of Brian Tracy, *The Psychology of Achievement.* It is an exceptionally well structured guide for setting and achieving your goals.

SPRING
S E A S O N

THE ACTIVITY IN OUR NEIGHBORHOOD changes in the Spring. There are more walkers, runners, people preparing their lawns for the warmer days, and even squirrels scurrying about after their Winter's nap. The trees, grass and flowers, lying dormant for a season, now also push forth buds and new sprouts.

Spring is a refreshing time. It is a time of new growth and new beginnings. It is a time that we also see more action as people and animals welcome the freshness and fragrances of this new cycle of life.

For the leader, the Spring of life is a time of learning, renewal and growth as well. It is during this time of the leader's life that they are aware that continual learning is the only way to prepare for the remaining seasons. It is through the many vehicles of education that the leader comes to terms with their need for knowledge and wisdom. And once they begin this Season, they soon realize they must put what they are learning into action.

As people, we learn in three very important ways. We learn by trial and error, through mentors and by way of formal education. This section is divided into these three parts. There is also a section that invites you to take what you are learning and use it to create new opportunities for your leadership and life.

For over two millennia, people from all walks of life have been calling us to become continual learners. It is an invitation as old as recorded time. It is also a prerequisite for leading in the 21st century. Failing in this area makes you inadequate to lead in the future.

RECOMMENDED BOOKS FOR THE SPRING SEASON:
An Invented Life: Reflections on Leadership and Change. Warren Bennis. Addison-Wesley: Reading, MA: 1993

The 7 Habits of Highly Effective People. Stephen Covey. Simon & Schuster: NY 1989

Jesus, CEO. Laurie Beth Jones. Hyperion: NY. 1992

Assessing Your Education

The direction in which education starts
a man will determine his future life.

—Plato
Greek philosopher & educator
(427-347 BC)

WE ALL HAVE SOME EDUCATIONAL HISTORY.
Whether formal education or learning from the "school of hard knocks," our lives to this moment have been defined by what we have learned and know.

Education comes in all forms—reading, experiences, watching others, or trial and error. Each plays a role in shaping the direction of our lives. Yet the most important point of all this education is not what knowledge you have accumulated to-date, but how this education has affected you and what you will choose to learn in the future.

I have witnessed the use of an activity that brings wonderful awareness to people. It is called a time-line. A time-line can represent any history, such as that of an organization, community, church, family or others. A personal educational time-line is extremely valuable in pinpointing activities or events in your life that define you as a person.

Constructing a personal educational time-line is rather simple. You start by drawing a horizontal line on a piece of paper. You label the left end of the line as age 0 and the right end as age 100 (because we all hope to live that long). You then make marks to represent five year increments from age 0 to 100.

Once you have completed this drawing, take time to reflect on what you learned or experienced during each of these five year time blocks. Either write or draw the events that influenced you as a person educationally. You might also consider what that event taught you about yourself or the world. Reflect on these events and learning experiences through your current age, making any notes of how one educational experience either led you to others or created barriers.

After working through your current age, consider what you think you will need to know in the future if you are to remain competitive, competent and ultimately reach your life goals. These reflections will become your educational plan. By setting this plan on paper, you can begin to undertake learning that is necessary for your development.

Every new day presents additional opportunities to learn. The question is: Do you consider your education complete or embrace the range of possibilities daily education offers? Making your choice will determine your destiny.

- What are the most important foundations you have from your formal learning experiences? What have you learned from other people? From trial and error?
- What is your most significant learning experience? What is the event in your life that taught you the most? What did you learn from it?
- In examining your educational background, what were barriers to learning for you? Are they still barriers?

Learn From Mistakes

A life spent in making mistakes is not only more honorable but more useful than a life spent doing nothing.

—George Bernard Shaw
Irish-born playwright
(1856-1950)

WE ARE A SOCIETY TERRIFIED of making mistakes. For many, making mistakes is a sign of weakness, lack of ability or incompetence. These attitudes towards mistakes shackle multitudes of people who might otherwise help solve a myriad of problems. Their mistakes might also add some zest to life. Ultimately, pride keeps us from taking risks that may in fact place our dreams within our grasp.

Shaw wrote it is more honorable, even noble, to make mistakes. From a practical standpoint, it is more useful than wishing life or circumstances would be different. Being willing to make mistakes readies you to enter the mainstream of life.

Years ago I read an article about a man that kept a "Mistake Log." The log contained notes from failed projects or circumstances that did not turn out as intended. This gentleman used the log as a personal teaching tool to increase productivity and the potential for success. Whenever he found himself faced with a new assignment or venture that had similarities to previous work, he read through the Mistake Log to predetermine what questions should be addressed ahead of time. By keeping notes and observations about past mistakes, this gentleman believed he was more productive in meeting new challenges because he could foresee barriers or obstacles.

A healthy perspective about making mistakes allows you to encounter life with fewer fears regarding how you will appear to others. On the other hand, being afraid to err relinquishes you to the grandstands as a spectator or keeps you from enjoying the opportunities that might come your way. Mistakes are a teaching tool. Embrace them.

• Are you afraid to make mistakes? Why? What keeps you sidelined in trying to fulfill your leadership dreams or mission?

• Write three things you are afraid to try because of your perspective of failure. Place one of these activities on your calendar to attempt in the next week. Keep a mental note of your feelings and how the event turned out after you did the activity.

Do Not Fear Failure

One who fears limits his activities.
Failure is only the opportunity to more
intelligently begin again.

—Henry Ford
Industrialist & automobile pioneer
(1863-1947)

FEAR IS DEBILITATING. It is natural to be afraid. But more often than not, our fears are unfounded. Researchers tell us that very few of our fears will ever become reality. Yet we allow these emotions to keep us from enjoying life or achieving success.

Fear of failure is universal. Being willing to fail can allow you to start anew with greater insight and competence for the task at hand. Remember, in taking risks you do not have to jump into the proverbial water with both feet to compensate for your fears. By taking calculated risks—even little steps—you can lead yourself to your goals. The security in calculated risks is that if you fail, you have not bet the farm. But no matter what, you must take some steps or you might miss the best opportunities life can offer.

I began writing over thirteen years ago. It started with accepting an assignment to write a small newsletter for a local civic organization. Just four pages in length, this newsletter gave me the opportunity to hone my writing and communication skills. My first nationally published article occurred eight years ago, due to the skills I had learned in writing the newsletter. From the critique and honing of my writing through calculated steps, I found greater opportunities for research, writing and publishing. If I had been afraid to write that small newsletter, I would never have discovered the excitement of writing for larger audiences.

Risk is a necessary part of your daily existence. Throughout the day, you take calculated risks like wearing a seat belt in your car, carrying an umbrella when it looks like rain or working to implement a plan at your work place.

Life risks are no different. They require you to take calculated measures to accomplish your goals. Your challenge is not to make those risks appear bigger than they are in reality. Your task is to cut the goal into manageable pieces, taking the necessary risks for reaching what you believe is your purpose.

• What are you afraid of in your career or life? Why are you afraid to risk, to make mistakes in your life, career or organization?

• What would be your personal reward if you triumphed over these fears and began taking some calculated risks?

Avoid Being a
Repeat Offender

*The measure of success is not whether you
have a tough problem to deal with, but whether
it's the same problem you had last year.*

—John Foster Dulles
Secretary of State for Eisenhower
(1888-1959)

HAVE YOU EVER NOTICED some people make the
same mistakes again and again? They face a problem, dilemma or temptation and repeatedly make the same decisions as
they have in the past. While there may be deeply personal
issues that force them to choose these decisions, we still
shake our heads and wonder why.

It may be easy to watch other people make repeated mistakes, but the question is do you, too, continue to make the
same choices? Do you find yourself encountering the same
situations, only to get the same results? Do you continue to
receive the same "stuff" from life year-in-and-year-out?

Golf is a wonderful sport. It really is an activity that is
much more than Rosey O'Donnel's observation of "old men
in ugly pants walking." Golf is interesting, not only for the
mental discipline required, but because it is an activity

where most players continue to stroke the ball the same way, over and over, year after year, hoping for a better score. Many golfers could actually improve their game significantly by slowing down and thinking about their shots as they take them. Through self talk about keeping their head down, eyes on the ball, and knees bent, they would hit the ball with greater precision. Or their game could significantly improve by taking a few lessons from an experienced golfer. My observation, however, is that many golfers perennially play from the hazards or continue shooting the same score because they choose not to take steps to improve their game.

Success is encountering the dilemmas of life, learning from them and using that information as a stepping stone to new opportunities. You will gradually move toward the prize of successful living when you choose to embrace your problems and take the steps to ensure they do not reoccur next year.

• What mistakes do you repeatedly make in your life? Why do you believe you continue to make the same choices again and again?

• What might you do in the future that will help you not make the same choices again? What will be your reward if you stop making the same mistakes?

Enlist Help

If you don't ask, the answer is always no.

—Pat Croce
Owner of the Philadelphia '76ers

FEAR IS A FORMIDABLE FOE. It paralyzes us from being who we desire to be or in starting what we long to undertake. Fear controls us for the simple fact that we have not reasoned through its attack nor considered the probability that its consequences will occur.

Fear also maligns because we are unwilling to ask. How often have you placed self limitation on your future or goals because you did not ask for assistance? How often have dreams gone to the grave because someone was fearful of rejection? Rejection is a powerful emotion, but its power is supernatural when we succumb to its illogical wooing.

Asking for assistance or consideration of an idea takes courage. Rejection has the tendency to conjure up our self-imposed inadequacies. Courage is the ingredient necessary for overpowering our self-doubts. The reality is it only takes about 60% courage over fear of rejection to accomplish your dreams or goals.

As an author, the fear of rejection was critical for me to overpower. I received rejection letters, almost from the start, when I turned in manuscripts to potential publishers. It would have been easier to give up writing to protect my ego and quench the emotion of rejection. But I have a passion for sharing my thoughts and reflection through the written word. The courage to place my manuscript in another envelop, ask people to read and critique my manuscripts, and take the necessary writing courses was more significant to me than the form letter rejection. If I had not pushed my fears aside and asked for help, I would have given up writing long ago.

The odds of obtaining your goals through the help of others increase when you are willing to dig deep to overcome the fear of rejection and vulnerability. Remember, if you are afraid to ask, your defeat will always be 100 percent.

- Why are you afraid to ask for assistance? What keeps you from asking people to hear your ideas or help you with your dreams? Is it pride, fear of rejection, fear of appearing incompetent?
- What might you gain if you overcome this fear of asking? What would be the rewards?

Remember the Elements of Past Successes

Constant success shows us but one side of the world. For as it surrounds us with friends who will tell us only our merits, so it silences those enemies from whom alone we can learn our defects.

—Charles Caleb Colton
English clergyman
(1780-1832)

I HAVE HEARD PEOPLE MUSE that human beings are afraid of success. While we may incessantly dream about success and all its trappings, we may inwardly be afraid to have it land squarely in our lap.

Successes, as well as mistakes, are significant teachers. The problem is that as we become successful, we may quit listening to those who would point out our defects. In reality, it is their bantering from the sidelines that may be more essential than the soothing voices of those around us.

About six years into my career, I received a promotion. The new assignment took on a much larger array of responsibilities, and I was excited about the recognition. Several months into this assignment, a friend and colleague came to my office to chat. After closing the door and some brief pleasantries, he candidly shared with me that I had changed. He went on to ask about my attitude and my newfound dictatorship in working with people. Needless to say, I was mortified. But I checked his observation with a few others and sure enough, I was different. His courage in sharing these insights with me not only saved my working relationships, but it returned me to the road of success that got me promoted in the first place.

In the transition to success, it is easy to forget how we made it and who we are. But those who continue to learn will make note of what was important before success and keep those secrets at hand.

• What ingredients can you identify in your own journey that you believe helped you become successful?

• Make a list of those elements that have helped you and place them in a conspicuous place to remind you daily of what is important to a healthy success.

Listen to Others

There is no better looking-glass than an old friend.

—Alexander Pope
English poet
(1688-1744)

THE **APOSTLE PAUL WROTE** that we cannot quite see the entire picture of our end desires as human beings. We are often like the person who sees their reflection in a mirror, then walks away and forgets their personal appearance. As human beings we are unable to remember what we had for lunch the day before, let alone the idiosyncrasies of our daily behaviors.

Whether you are a leader or just desiring to live with purpose, you need mentors and friends. These people in your life provide the looking-glass needed to live wholly. Mentors and friends will provide you with a self-view you can never fully get alone, as long as you are willing to listen honestly and intently.

Mentors are liberators. We will experience growth and find insight if we intently listen to the words of mentors. The liberation from mentors comes in three ways. First, a mentor is an encourager. Real mentors encourage us to take risks, give our best efforts and develop a sound moral character. Mentors never accept adequate work or a shading of the truth, but challenge us to live to our full potential.

Second, mentors tell the truth about our flaws. There is an old adage that expresses this mentoring role. The adage says, "If one person tells you you are a horse, disregard their comments. If two people tell you you are a horse, laugh at the suggestion. But if ten people tell you you are a horse, you should buy a saddle." The critique of a mentor has the power of ten. Listen to them.

Finally, mentors free us to fly. Through their insight, encouragement and involvement in our lives, we become what we were created to be. Mentors come to us as one who opens the door for a caged bird, allowing it to soar.

Mentors are also important because they expect the best from us in all situations. It is true we become like the people we associate with on a regular basis. If they are negative and cynical, they will drag us to the lowest level of expectation about ourselves and others. But if our associates are positive, upbeat and expect the best for life, we will also become positive and affirming of what life has to offer. Good mentors want the best for us. Seek their positive expectations of you.

The latest trend in performance review is the 360 perspective, trusting others to tell us where we need improvement. While this may be a much needed tool in our time, an old, true and utterly honest friend might really be all you need.

• Do you have a mentor or someone that is your looking glass? Who are they? What do they provide for you in helping you become the person you desire to be?

• If you do not have a mentor or good friend, whom would you like to have as a friend in your life? What might you do to begin to develop that friendship? Remember, if you don't ask them, their response is always No!

Find a Mentor

*In life you throw a ball. You hope it will
reach a wall and bounce back so you can
throw it again. You hope your friends will
provide the wall.*

—Pablo Picasso
Spanish-born painter
(1881-1973)

PLAYING BALL AGAINST A WALL CAN BE FUN. But
it also can become monotonous. Back and forth with the
same consistency, over and over again, without change.

Mentors and friends provide for us a wall that gives some
variety to the game. A little faster return, maybe a spin on
the ball, possibly a high lob changes the pace of life. These
life companions give us a dimension of diversity that we
alone can never know.

One of my mentors first appeared in my class with his
wife in tow. He was a burly man, a Viet Nam veteran, who
had created his own life. Beginning his career as a plumber,
he had worked his way into management and ultimately into
computer programming and consulting for a large community school corporation. As he sat down in a chair, he looked
the class over with a cocked eyebrow and declared, "You can
socialize with my wife, but that's not for me."

All of us were unsure of this mountainous man from the very start. He always seemed to growl or huff and many people disliked him immediately. But hidden beneath that rough exterior was a man who loved his family deeply and cherished his wife. He was also always seeking insights about life, love and serving others. Below that intimidating frame was a man sensitive to others.

In the following years, Dirk became a friend who did not take pat answers or off the cuff responses as legitimate. He was a challenging man who demanded honesty from himself and others. Occasionally his inquisitiveness and need for discussion brought him to our doorstep in the late evening hours because he wanted to talk while the reflections were still fresh on his mind.

It was October when we learned Dirk had liver cancer. He took the news well, but nevertheless began to set in motion the care his family would need if he passed away. It was also the point at which our friendship became deeper and more honest as we struggled together with this disease.

In the early days of March, our fifteen year old daughter shared with my wife and me she was pregnant. I began to loose control of my dreams and desires for our family and my own life. I found it easy to drop out of sight from my normal activities, but Dirk would not let me get away. This friend found me, and challenged me to accept what life presented and move to wholeness.

Dirk's blunt honesty crushed me one night during a visit to the hospital where he was having chemotherapy. He put his patented drop look on me, cocked his eyebrow and said, "You are a blessed person to see life coming into the world. I may not live long. You have an opportunity to see a new beginning in this grandchild." I was angry and hurt that he would broach the subject, especially in front of others.

But Dirk was the friend who bounced the ball back to me when I had thrown it into the darkness. In the months after my hospital visit, we talked of life, the future, forgiveness and love. In the few days prior to his death, we silently sat and held hands, sharing what goodness could come from such desperate times.

I threw a ball and a burly, sometimes coarse and tough man, caught the ball and bounced it back. We were fortunate to have shared life and death together. Your life, too, will be blessed beyond measure if you encounter such a friend.

- If you took a risk, what might you ask your mentor or friend to tell you about yourself that would help you improve even 10%? Are you willing to take the risk for the sake of improvement? Why or why not?
- Are you willing to find a friend—just one—who can help you become all you were created to be?

Is Education a Part of Your Success?

Education is not preparation for life.
Education is life itself.

—John Dewey, American
philosopher & educator
(1859-1952)

OXYGEN KEEPS YOU ALIVE. Without this critical element, you will not survive more than a dozen minutes.

Education is also critical to your life. Without it, you will die intellectually. The problem with education, however, is you can live for a few months or even years without it. But as surely as you will succumb to death from lack of oxygen, you will also eventually die mentally by not feeding your mind.

There was never a time to believe that education can stop at some predetermined point in your life. With information exploding, work complexities mounting, or the global village becoming the way of life, you must stay immersed in the waters of education, reading and training. Dr. Robert Bjork of UCLA says we are self-illusionary about what we know. By this, Dr. Bjork means you will no longer study, practice or acquire more skills when you think or feel you know all there is to know about a subject. This self-delusion causes you to stop the constant pursuit of learning. And when you stop learning, your memories fade and you quickly become obsolete, both now and in the 21st century.

Your challenge is not to create educational delusion but to proactively focus on constant learning. Education and learning not only prepare you to live more fully and successfully, but they ultimately will sustain your life and future.

• Do you believe education is essential for all your life? Why or why not?

• Continual, long-term education is critical to your success. What are you currently doing to stay mentally alert through learning? List what you are doing. Next to these activities, note how much time every week you spend in learning.

Nourish Your Mind Continually

They know enough who know how to learn.

—Henry Brooks Adams
The Education of Henry Brooks
American historian
(1838-1918)

A **MIXTURE OF NITROGEN,** phosphorous and good rich soil provides needed nutrients for fertilizing and growing strong, healthy plants. Just as all living things need nourishment, leaders realize that the feeding of their minds and hearts is important to their personal influence and readiness for the future. In the simplest terms, leaders are continual learners. As our world becomes more complex, the challenge will be for leaders to remain adaptable and flexible through learning.

Continual learning, whether through structured courses or through personal reading patterns, is imperative if you are to grow. The quiet aspect of learning is that it is not considered an urgent activity, but it is most critical to your future. With a humble voice, the call to learning is often drowned out by time wasters, the pressures of the day and the anxiety of the present. These distractions snuff out the long-term preparedness needed to become effective leaders and people.

Constant learning does not happen with the occasional reading of a magazine, journal or the hottest management book. Continual learning is hard work, often requiring years to master and store the material necessary to make good leadership and personal decisions.

When all is said and done, leaders nourish their minds because they know a prepared mind leads toward success. An educated mind also leads you to fulfilling your vision and seeing the opportunities not always evident at first glance toward the mountains of existing research and data. Through constant learning, effective leaders keep themselves open to the massive ocean of possibilities.

In the end, learning is not simply about amassing knowledge for knowledge's sake. Your education is really about learning, unlearning and relearning what is necessary to be successful in both leadership and life. But all your knowledge is worthless if it is not translated into action. Ultimately, it is through the journey of continual learning that you begin to see the world with new eyes and are able to meet its myriad of problems with a stronger insight for solutions.

• Who is responsible for your education? Are you personally responsible for your learning and education or do you believe it is the duty of your organization or someone else to teach you? Why?

• Do you make excuses for not learning? What are they and why do you persist in making them?

Making Learning a Priority

The greater the obstacle the greater the glory in overcoming it.

—Jean Baptiste Moliere
French playwright
(1622-1673)

HAYSTACKS STAND AS MINIATURE MOUNTAINS in crowded barnyards. That mental picture is not unlike the reading mounds found in offices everywhere. It is bewildering to sit before these growing heaps of magazines, books or data. How can you gain control of this never ending stream of information? The simplest method for gaining control of this formidable educational obstacle is found in a riddle. The riddle asks, "How do you eat an elephant?" The answer is, "One bite at a time." You can reduce this information mountain into bite size pieces through some simple and proactive reading activities.

Reading or any learning is a matter of choice. While reading does take time, it can be accomplished by setting it as a priority. Reading time does not have to be a burden. By rearranging some time slots available in the course of a week, you will gain the needed time for reading and study. Over the past twenty years, I have found some painless methods for taking a bite out of the reading overload. While the stacks may grow rapidly at times, taking a few minutes every day allows you to overcome the influx of paper.

Ever take a friend to lunch? That is your friend, a book. Instead of spending every lunch hour with friends or other business contacts, make a lunch date once a week with a book. In a matter of no time, you will have finished a book and reduced your anxiety about information overload.

But if you desire to have lunch with friends and read, consider forming a reading group. Not only will you have the fellowship of the lunch time, but you will have the accountability of reading a book with others. Being involved in a reading group is stimulating, particularly as you share together with others the contents of the book and the ideas it presents. Creativity, insight and regeneration are wonderful byproducts of this time spent with friends and a book.

Getting out of bed ½ hour earlier each morning will reward you with 23 eight-hour days for reading each year. Over a year's time, those days alone are enough to keep you abreast of the best thinking and data produced in your profession or in your life.

Americans spend nearly 30 hours a week watching television. With so much time spent on this activity, it is no wonder reading mountains grow. Instead of snuggling up with the remote control, take a book or magazine in hand while letting the TV fade to black one hour sooner each night. That one hour will give you 45 eight-hour days of reading each year.

Ever wait in an office and stare at those three-year old magazines available for your enjoyment? Instead of zoning out in these moments, photocopy articles from your reading stack, and take them with you. These articles can be taken on planes, trains and automobiles for those moments when you have to wait.

The automobile is one of the world's marvelous transportation inventions—and educational tools. The commute to and from your workplace can become an endless learning library by using the cassette player in your car. You can learn a language, listen to entire books or be inspired by a plethora of motivational speakers in the commuting time to work or in running errands. My work commute totals 30 minutes every day. In that time span, I gain 16 eight-hour learning days while stopping, starting or turning on red.

We make appointments for everything. We place notes on our calendars for vacations, little league games and meetings, yet we neglect to make appointments for learning. Reading, too, demands an appointment. Setting appointments with yourself to read helps to overpower the stacks of materials that quickly accumulate. The essential part of this appointment, however, is to treat it like any other appointment—without interruption.

My son taught me another valuable tool for continual learning. It is called "Thinking Thursday." As a third grader, my son was excited about this particular day because it was set aside for learning that was fun as well as challenging. I have used Thinking Thursday throughout my career. It is a day when I read, reflect on projects or learn about new products and services. What I have come to realize in this activity is most of the world values the appearance of busyness and not the time of proactive thinking and learning. Nevertheless, place Thinking Thursday on your calendar and watch the results.

Increasing your knowledge and skill level cannot happen if you continue to make excuses for your learning. Leaders realize if there is time to watch television or participate in a host of other activities, there is time for learning through reading. Leadership education does not happen by chance. It happens by choice.

- What are the identifiable moments in your day that could be used for reading and learning?
- Attend proactively to your reading. Try choosing a variety of learning materials that will keep you aware of the larger world happenings. Balance your learning by choosing a comprehensive newspaper, a news magazine, a cultural magazine, technology readings, a business magazine and a global events magazine (like World Press Review). Reading from each category will keep you aware of our planet's issues.

Memory: Keeping Your Mind Active

Iron rusts from disuse, stagnant water loses its purity, and in cold weather becomes frozen; even so does inaction sap the vigor of the mind.

—Leonardo Da Vinci
Florentine painter & inventor
(1452-1519)

OUR MEMORIES ARE CRITICAL for encountering the world. We are only able to read, solve math problems, drive a car or find our way home because we have stored images and patterns in our memories. All our behaviors are influenced by what is stored in our memory and what we can recall at the appropriate time.

Just as memory and active use of your mind allows you to encounter the world, so effective leaders store the best leadership and learning experiences in memory for guiding their future performance. These individuals have literally used their mind to pay attention, practice, learn and master leadership and character ingredients that offer effectiveness when they are called upon to lead.

Actively paying attention determines what goes into memory and what comes out. When you use your mind to actively process your experiences and learning, you store information that will be useful to you in the appropriate setting. You also keep your mind vigorous when you constantly practice and review what you are learning. Through this practice—and even overlearning—your mind makes successful leadership, character and vision memories stronger, so that when your leadership or character is needed, you will not falter in the heat of battle.

Experts in memory research write that memory is basically learning. If you are to be an effective leader, it is imperative that you make learning, relearning and continual learning your priority. In the field of memory research one prescription seems to be universal: you remember more when the degree of learning is great. Keeping your mind active provides the best chance of performing well as a leader and as a person.

Peter Senge of the Society of Organizational Learning recently wrote that the most effective learning consists of out of the box experiences, coupled with constant practice.

> How do you learn, say, team-based product development? The same way you learn to write or to play the piano or to perfect your golf stroke—you practice. You never reach the end. No matter how much you write, play the piano, or golf, you're aware how much better you can get. You have to exploit opportunities in people's daily experience to continually enhance their capacities—which is really all that learning means.

Continual learning, mentally storing experience patterns and keeping your mind active, does not happen by occasionally reading magazines, journals, or the hottest management books. Continual learning is proactive work, often requiring years to master and mentally store experience patterns that can be recalled when needed. Dr. Eugene Griessman, author of *The Path to Achievement*, shares that Chess Grand Masters learn and relearn chess patterns and combinations over a period of 15 years before they win their first world title. Applying leadership and character lessons through memory recall takes hours and years of practicing, learning and concentrating if you are to succeed.

Learning leadership or any knowledge is essential if you are to transform your family, organization and community. Your challenge is to practice, learn, and review your leadership and character elements frequently. Just as actively learning and practicing are linked to remembering, likewise not practicing and discontinuing learning contribute directly to forgetting what you have already learned. Without practice, you are in danger of forgetting. While you may be able to explain the concept of addition or for that matter leadership to someone else, you can't add or perform effectively if you haven't practiced and practiced.

One of the most powerful tools on this planet is your mind. But unless you actively use it, your mind will atrophy like any muscle of your body.

• Do you keep your mind active through regular learning opportunities? What are they and how are they keeping your mind alert?

• What are you learning but not practicing? What will you do immediately to set a time to practice your newfound knowledge?

Participate in
the Dialogue

All education is a continuous dialogue—
questions and answers that pursue every
problem to the horizon.

—William O. Douglas
U.S. Supreme Court Justice
(1898-1980)

EDUCATION IS A DIALOGUE. It is a continual seeking
and finding of solutions to problems that we encounter
throughout life. Successful people continually work to sort
out what they are learning in order to understand the bigger
picture, rather than the antidote for the moment.

Our learning is most valuable when we spend time assess-
ing situations and finding the relationships that might exist
between various scenarios. We often fail to see larger solutions
to problems because we do not assess and compare similarities
that might exist between several sets of circumstances.

Dr. Brian Ross of the University of Michigan believes
part of our intellectual barrier comes as a result of making
superficial associations between situations, instead of looking
for deeper connections. Dr. Ross calls this deeper investigation "cross domain transfer." Ross explains cross domain

transfer when he shares, "you are more likely to remember past experiences of fixing a clogged pipe when repairing new plumbing problems, rather than what you might know about electricity." By this Ross means as humans we segment our learning and compartmentalize what we know. Cross domain transfer is thus trying to understand the similarities between plumbing problems and the laws of electricity. While it is harder to do, you may view a clogged pipe as a restriction of flow which would allow you to use what you also know about the flow of electricity. Real insight and innovation can emerge when you diligently dialogue about the relationships between plumbing and electricity. Overcoming our tendency to compartmentalize or segment information may actually provide us with insight we may never have grasped otherwise.

While it is harder and takes more time for sorting through relationships between problems, it will teach you there may be overarching principles governing a host of problems you encounter. By critically thinking about relationships, you may begin to see patterns or nuances of situations that might apply to other issues you face. It is this constant dialogue—internally and with others—that permits you to see old problems with new understanding.

This educational dialogue takes intention and work to make it effective. It will also require that you think outside the box when presented with problems or issues that need new perspectives. We all have comfort zones when working with problems. When we are in these zones, we rely on established ideas or behaviors to get us through circumstances. But new insight and innovation, as Stephen Covey observed, comes not from a "break through," but from a "break with" established ways of doing things.

I teach a course on archaeology and Ancient Near Eastern History. On the first class day of the semester, I tell students to read the business classic, The Fifth Discipline, by Peter Senge. Now what does this business book have to do with ancient history? The connection is that the book discusses systems and processes that help us make decisions. That concept is critical to understanding history. The frustration in teaching history is that students often believe an event had to turn out as we know it because that is how the textbook explains it. But the reality is that people lived in their own contexts, in their own times, with their own ambitions and made decisions based on a host of nuances lost to us. I believe our task as history students is to understand there may have been another outcome recorded in our books if people made different decisions based on different assumptions. My teaching role is to help students see the range of historical possibilities and to challenge students to consider how their decisions and actions will alter the future. It is my challenge to help students understand how "cross domain transfer" might actually assist them in making the wisest possible decisions.

You have solutions to your problems. At issue is that you may not have taken the time to think critically or had a dialogue with yourself or others outside your comfort zone about those solutions. Constant mental dialogue sees the solution on the horizon and recognizes the path for meeting it face-to-face.

• Are you spending time dialoguing across disciplines to find solutions? Are you keeping your mind critically alert to possibilities outside your circle of responsibility?

• Try reading or working with others unlike yourself or different from your career. Pay attention to how they solve problems or approach issues. Look for patterns that might assist you in finding solutions to the issues you face in your workplace.

Taking Off
Your Blinders

Only the educated are free.

—Epictetus, *Discourses*
Greek stoic philosopher
(AD 60-117)

WE ARE A CULTURE that protects our freedom. Whether personal freedom or that claimed by a group, we bristle if someone treads on our rights. The problem is we may be protecting some of these freedoms out of ignorance. Prejudices, stereotyping, and mass generalizations diminish the liberties of others. Many of these limitations could be removed if we were willing to become educated in order to be free.

I grew up within miles of the Amish communities of Ohio. As a young boy, I remember watching the horse drawn carriages transport people across rural areas to their destinations. The horses always wore blinders. I later learned that blinders are necessary to keep the horse focused on what is straight ahead. These small leather flaps do not allow the horse to see anything to either side, so that they are not startled by their surroundings. With blinders on, these beasts methodically and dutifully walk to their destination.

Looking down the tunnel of reduced peripheral vision is necessary for keeping these animals and their passengers safe, but blinders on people prevent us from seeing the world. Education is not just about knowing something. It is about taking off the blinders to the larger issues in the world. When we absorb and understand what we learn, we can take away the generalizations about others or situations. This breaking down of barriers leads us to greater freedom and opportunity. It also helps us in making new decisions about old paradigms. Removing educational blinders opens your world to greater perspectives and possibilities than you might have ever imagined.

You do have a choice about freedom. The question is, "Are you willing to become educated so that you might be free?"

• What are the prejudices or stereotypes you have about people, places, social issues, business issues, or any other situations you may have encountered in life?

• Where do you have limited knowledge about these issues? What will you need to know to make better decisions and overcome your prejudices?

What Don't
You Know?

Ignorance is the night of the mind, a
night without moon or stars.

—Confucius
Chinese philosopher
(551-479 BC)

NOT KNOWING THAT WE DO NOT KNOW is a dangerous place. As a moonless night cannot provide light for a journey in the darkness, so ignorance shrouds us from seeing potential and opportunities that lie before us.

Conversely, the awareness that our knowledge is limited, restricting or incomplete is the beginning of wisdom. If we confess our limited knowledge, we are ready to begin the journey toward wisdom. Our adventures and discoveries through learning are only confined by our willingness or lack thereof to experience the universe. Our pursuit must be to know more tomorrow than we know today.

One of the most exciting classrooms you have available is the organization in which you work. It is a place that can allow you to grow and know the world in a much larger way than ever before. There are boundless avenues for daily learning in your organization. For example, learn products or services in your company that you do not work with daily, or cross train in another department. You might also volunteer for assignments or work on committees where you can learn skills of team building, negotiation or conflict resolution. Your learning opportunities are only as limited as your imagination.

I have also learned that reading groups open my mind to greater possibilities. It is easy to form a reading group. It is simply a matter of finding others who want to learn, asking them to read a book together, and then taking the time to discuss the contents of the book. I have been a part of a reading group in my workplace. The insights and reflection gained from others were energizing. Through that biweekly meeting, I learned about people, their assignments, the effects of my decisions on their work and how to be a better citizen of my institution.

If you admit there is much you do not know about the world, every waking minute is a learning opportunity. If you sincerely desire to move from ignorance to wisdom, you will find imaginative ways to use this entire planet as your classroom.

- What skills, knowledge or abilities must be honed in your life if your leadership, your career or your personal life is to grow?
- What do you not know but need to know in order to be a more effective leader and achieve your life mission?
- What are some ways the whole earth might be your classroom? What could you learn by taking time to seek opportunities to understand what others do in your organization?
- For information on starting a reading group, review the web site at www.mgeneral.com/1-lines/98-lines/022198li.htm

Learning Shouldn't Stop on Graduation Day

The wisest mind hath something yet to learn.

—George Santayana
Spanish-born philosopher & author
(1863-1952)

ONE OF THE GREAT AMERICAN TRAGEDIES is believing we are finished with our education when we graduate from high school or college. For many, education and learning are means to an end instead of the beginning to a never ending journey.

Leaders are perpetual learners. They are cognizant that they must continue to learn throughout all their lives. For leaders, a diploma is simply the gateway to new adventures for the mind. And in the end, they come to experience that learning is the beginning of wisdom.

I keep the Table of Contents to the book *The Life Time Reading Plan* in my day planner. Editor Clifton Fadiman has compiled in this book a series of readings from a cross section of classic Western literature. The editor invites you to spend your lifetime learning wisdom through some of the greatest literature in the history of the world. As Fadiman shares, these books are intended to be a part of your whole life, no matter your age. "They can be a major experience, a source of continuous internal growth. . . . These authors are life companions. Once part of you, they work in and on and with you until you die." Whether it is Homer, Herodatus, Hemmingway or Durant, the challenge is to find wisdom for today through a play, history, poem or autobiography of yesteryear.

I have read many of these works in the course of the twenty five years since my high school graduation. It never ceases to amaze and thrill me that the wisdom of the past is relevant for me today. I have grown as a leader and human being by taking the time to become friends with the world's greatest minds. While it does take proactive use of my time, I am the richer for having been associated with great literature. These works, as Fadiman observes, "help us avoid mental bankruptcy."

Borrow Fadiman's book on your next visit to the public library. It is a pearl of great price. In addition to Fadiman's book, I would also encourage you to read the works listed below. They may not be considered classics yet, but they will open your mind to fresh perspectives on the world.

Habits of the Heart. Robert Bellah. Harper & Row Publishers: NY 1986

Collaborative Leadership. David Chrislip. Jossey-Bass: San Francisco 1994

Small is Beautiful: Economics as if People Mattered. EF Schumacher. Harper & Row: NY 1973

Future Edge. Joel Barker. William Morrow: NY 1992

Reinventing Leadership: Warren Bennis & Robert Townsend. William Morrow: NY 1995

Seeker & Servant. Robert Greenleaf. Larry Spears, Editor. Jossey-Bass: San Francisco 1996

Life Together. Dietrich Bonhoffer. Harper Collins: NY 1954

When the Canary Stops Singing. Pat Barrentine. Berrett Koehler: San Francisco 1993

The Fifth Discipline. Peter Senge. Doubleday: NY 1990

A New Paradigm of Leadership: Visions of Excellence for 21st Century Organizations. Ken Shelton, editor. Executive Excellence Publishing: Provo, UT. 1997

• Set proactive time to read the classics of Fadiman's book. They are challenging reading but are worthwhile in presenting you with an undiscovered world waiting inside of you.

• While you read, ask yourself, "What is this book telling me that I did not know or needed to know?" The book will come alive when you have a dialogue with yourself and the writer.

New Eyes for New Vision

*The real voyage of discovery consists
not in seeking new lands, but in seeing with
new eyes.*

—Marcel Proust
French novelist
(1871-1922)

A **TRIP TO ISRAEL REVEALED** a land I knew but did
not know. I have been reading Bible stories all my life and
learned about the history of Israel during my college days.
Yet traveling in that country showed me that my preconcep-
tions were askew. In seeing the land, I had new connections.
For the first time, those decades of stories took on new mean-
ings as I saw them through new experiences.

In my journey throughout Israel, I realized that it is a
land of great contrasts. The northern countryside is lush and
beautiful in Galilee and yet barren and desert only a few
hours south at the Dead Sea. I also realized that Jesus spent
most of his ministry in an area roughly four kilometers
between Tiberias and Capernaum. My readings and study
now have new significance and deeper insights because I
experienced this ancient land with new eyes.

Continual learning and education, coupled with new experiences, help you see your old world from a new perspective. An enlightened mind, stretched with new ideas, cannot go back to its original shape. It is as T. S. Eliot wrote, "We shall not cease from exploration and the end of all our exploring will be to arrive where we started and know the place for the first time."

- What are you really seeing for the first time?
- How have these new insights affected you?
- What are you doing differently because of seeing with new eyes?
- What adventure, reading or study might you undertake that would help you to better understand your current situation or your life dreams?

Education Fosters
Intuitive Creativity

But Farmer Hoggett knew that little ideas that tickled, nagged and refused to go away should never be ignored. For in them lay seeds of destiny.

—*Babe* (The movie)
Universal Studios
(1996)

I HAVE HEARD PEOPLE SAY MANY TIMES, "I thought about that idea." or "Look at that invention. I thought of it—I could be rich!" We have all had that experience. We may even be the person saying it.

An educated mind is like radar to the possibilities lying dormant in the universe. Edison believed inventions are everywhere in the airwaves. Our challenge is being a radio receiver that allows us to pick them from the air.

Education and learning allow you to be a radio receiver, taking in all the great ideas available to humanity. And once you are receptive to what is out there, it takes your perseverance not to let those ideas be smothered. Remember, there are big people with small minds that can become barriers to your ideas and dreams. Sometimes it will require your tenacity to forge ahead, particularly in the face of public ridicule.

An important concept I teach my history students is "objectified thought." This concept states that the tangible artifacts we take from the ground archaeologically or use every day are merely a person's ideas formed into tangible objects. Simply put, a pencil you hold in your hand is an extension of your index finger that was once used to write in the sand. But since writing in the sand is not permanent, someone thought about writing with a stick with charcoal, that became a stylus for writing on clay, that ultimately became a lead pencil. Those that invented or improved these original thoughts are not necessarily classified as genius. But they can be classified as inquisitive minds who coupled their insights with action.

If you get an idea that tickles and refuses to go away, don't fight its pull or subdue its calling. For in those ideas "lay the seeds of destiny."

• What ideas have you been incubating for some time that could turn out to be your destiny? Make a list of them. Next to each of them, write what you need to know to make them a reality, which one(s) will receive your priority, and when you will start work on each idea.

• As force of habit, create an idea log. Whenever you have an idea or creative thought, write it down with a date, what you need to know and how it fits with your mission and goals. Spend time weekly working these ideas into your annual planning.

• Purchase or rent the movie, *Babe*. It is a delightful children's movie with wonderful adult themes throughout. Watch it and ponder its messages.

Recover Your Childhood Curiosity

The important thing is not to stop questioning. Curiosity has its own reason for existing.

—Albert Einstein
German-born physicist &
Nobel Prize laureate
(1879-1955)

I **DISLIKE THE PHRASE,** "curiosity kills the cat." By uttering that phrase, we easily fall victim to believing curiosity is a bad thing. Even Webster defines curiosity as a meddling or inquisitiveness that is bothersome and selfish.

Healthy curiosity is essential for discovery and innovation. The "What if . . ." Hewlett Packard commercials are the sum of what healthy curiosity can reveal. Being curious focuses on your desire to know. It is also the foundation for life-long learning.

Curiosity is about inquiring, researching and asking questions to ideas or "What ifs . . . " that are important to you. Curious investigation and critical thinking may also reveal to you new vistas that lead to problem solving, new innovations or breakthroughs, both personally and organizationally.

It's been said before that children are born question marks and by adulthood they become periods, knowing what is necessary to know and no more. Spending time with a small child will help you understand the mind-set needed for healthy curiosity.

Children want to experience how the world works. It is the first time they are experiencing the wonders of life, nature, their bodies and relationships with others. Questions like, "Why is salt salty?" or "Do fish drink water?" or "Can a worm lay on its back?" are the stuff of observation, critical thinking, problem solving and self education.

Healthy curiosity is believing there is an awesome quality to life just waiting to be enjoyed. Reviving that inquisitiveness in yourself can bring new perspectives to your world. Destroying that marvel of a child is also a sin.

• What keeps you from being curious? Do you believe curiosity kills the cat?

• Do the curious questions of children bother you or are they opportunities to develop relationships, spark learning and encounter the awesomeness of the universe?

Principled Intuition

*There is something in our minds like
sunshine and weather, which is not under
our control. When I write, the best things
come to me from I know not where.*

—Georg Christoph Licthenberg
German physicist & satirist
(1742-1799)

HAVE YOU EVER SENSED that a critical action plan or
project didn't seem right? And when all the facts were in,
you were correct in your hunch?

Since ancient times, people have been aware there is a
sense that tells us to take a different course, try another
method, or look at the situation again. From seers and mys-
tics to philosophers, many people have tried to explain intuition—that sense of knowing beyond what is seen.
Cultivating our feelings and our hunches of intuition can
enhance our development, especially if they are rooted in
timeless principles and values.

Principled intuition helps you to look, listen, touch and
feel the direction of your life to make sure it is on course to
accomplish the greatest good for all. If your desire is to be of
service, you must "see" beyond facts and figures.

You can benefit from developing your intuition. The key is remembering that intuition is not a mystical sixth sense but an ability to draw conclusions—whether they are right or wrong. Intuition is a means of subconsciously sorting and integrating perceived factors into an impression that can guide your behavior.

Intuition has practical application. Following intense focus on an idea or issue, intuitive insight can naturally flow. Ultimately a light bulb of new understanding emerges from the far recesses of your mind.

While you may not be aware of your intuitive insights, intuition can be developed. One way to develop intuition is to reflect on what people say and do. Intuition is connecting the subtle clues people provide through communication and behavior.

Another activity is watching for the interdependency of events and outcomes. Too often, we are caught in the mindset that one event comes from one sole and isolated action. But heightening your alertness and receptivity to the whole event will demonstrate that events have a multitude of influences at their core. If you are not open to the whole scenario, the intuitive insights cannot be gleaned.

Third, intuition can be increased by critical reading. An educated, aware mind is more open to subtleties. And the reading should be widespread, not just limited to your chosen field. The interplay of information from other fields of study provides intuitive exploration.

A fourth practice is reflecting and asking questions of the event that is happening to you now. You must ask questions such as: What is the purpose of this event? What do I see in the situation?

By asking questions, dialoguing with yourself and others, and taking time for reflection, you become more receptive to the nuances. Out of these ponderings of the problems come the magical flashes of insight.

Finally, intuition can be developed by working at understanding and grasping patterns which emerge from what we read, question and discuss. Intuitive insight sees the patterns and range of possibilities amid the mountains of data. These moments of discovery will lead you into new opportunities and new challenges.

Principled intuition asks you to take action. Without action, your discernment is of little use. Intuition without action is nothing more than a curious feeling or a fleeting hunch. But principled intuition, coupled with action, may mean legacy building of enormous proportions.

* Are you aware of the subtleties of behavior, language, tone of voice, eye movements or other nonverbal communications given by others?

* Do you look for interdependency of information and data, particularly if it is from seemingly unrelated disciplines?

* When you read, do you have a conversation with the author about his or her ideas, insights, or statements, or do you just accept what he or she writes?

Learn in order to Serve

> . . . for attaining wisdom and discipline; for providing words of insight; for acquiring a disciplined and prudent life, doing what is right and just and fair; for giving prudence to the simple, knowledge and discretion to the young—let the wise listen and add to their learning, and let the discerning get guidance. . . .
>
> —Proverbs of Solomon (the Prologue)
> *The Bible*, Proverbs 1:1-5

GETTING AND GIVING is the essence of all learning. When we learn, we mentally get what is necessary for understanding the world and then give that knowledge in tangible ways to improve its condition. It is through this ebb and flow of getting and giving that we obtain the wisdom that leads to personal and community well-being.

Attaining knowledge and wisdom are not end products. Acquiring life knowledge is ultimately for moral development, purposeful living and well-being. Through learning, you become disciplined by the rigors of questioning, researching and exploration. If you are attentive to the discipline inherent in quality learning, you can translate that skill to other areas of your life. But a surprising aspect in getting wisdom is the production of a prudent life.

Prudence is not a word we are used to hearing, let alone applying. Prudence is being careful to avoid errors in judgment so that well-being is the long term result. Two characteristics emerge from our learning when we live prudently.

First, a prudent person makes sacrifices in the present to ensure a successful future. Prudent people do not simply look ahead and dream about a successful and wonderful life. When you live prudently, you see the desired future and then begin creating that desired vision through your actions. Quite often, the future can only be successful if you are willing to delay gratification of the present so that the future might be the best possible.

A prudent person also makes sound judgments. They have learned that practical wisdom and good decision making are essential for well-being. Prudent people ask questions about what makes for success and then actively find answers to their inquiry. They never leave choices among possible options to fate.

Discernment is a part of sound decision making. We discern between options by critically thinking through what each presents. Discernment is like a boat rudder. It allows you to steer between all the choices presented, while choosing those that lead you to the harbor of your personal mission. Without discernment, it is easy to pick what looks like the harbor but is in reality a jagged shoal that sinks our dreams.

Once we attain understanding through our critical questioning and discipline, we are obligated to share our insights in tangible ways. A wise person displays understanding by being right, fair and just. They are willing to spend the necessary efforts to make good decisions about a matter—never providing a rash response to a situation that requires their best thinking. By having a mind-set of justice, they desire to know the nuances of a matter from all involved parties before they express their opinion or decision.

We also share wisdom when we teach others how to live a disciplined and prudent life. People are often caught in the glamour of quick fixes for their problems. But wise people share with others how to find real and lasting well-being by sacrificing now for a richer life to come.

Finally, getting wisdom reminds us to give ourselves to mentoring youth. Learning for ourselves and for our sole profit is a deep self-centeredness. Learning should open our minds and hearts to teaching, to sharing a path with our children that will also lead them to success.

People who learn and become wise know and listen. Knowing is not about what is in your head. Knowing is about what is both in your head and in your heart. This combination will provide the arena for making the right life choices. Wisdom is also about listening. The wise do not listen just with their ears. The wise person takes what comes into their ears and transfers that understanding to their hands and feet through action.

It is not complicated to be wise. But it does take a willing heart and hard work to make it real.

- Are you disciplined in your learning? Do you actively address learning or just wait for it to happen?
- Are you willing to sacrifice some pleasures or possessions now for a better result in the future? Why or why not?
- Are you discerning? Do you spend time critically thinking through options presented to you or do you take the option that presents the best first impression?
- Do you spend time sharing through mentoring what life is teaching you? Do you believe mentoring relationships are worthwhile or a drain on your personal time?

Seek Wisdom

Wisdom is the highest virtue, and it has in it four other virtues; of which one is prudence, another temperance, the third fortitude, the fourth justice.

—Boethius
Roman philosopher, statesman &
Christian theologian
(480-525)

WISDOM HAS BEEN SOUGHT by people for millennia. From wise men and women, we have desired an utterance that would bring clarity, meaning, peace, or contentment to our lives. Even today many still seek wisdom to make sense of work, self or life.

Wisdom is not about uncovering hidden mysteries, but is a willingness to reflect, observe, and reason about the experiences we encounter or see in the world. Through reflection, discussion and self-dialogue, the wise assess what is of most value and apply those lessons to everyday existence. Seeking wisdom is a patient sorting out of what brings an abundant life.

The goal of wisdom is to bring quality and principle to your life, through a balance of how you live and relate with others. The knowledge gained from your reflection is not an end alone, but a way to learn how to live with satisfaction, contentment, balance, and moral order.

Wisdom is available to anyone willing to discern and see what others miss as they watch the world go by. To be wise is to hear not with your ears alone, but with your intellect and heart. This listening is done to glean truth that will shed light on your questions about success, well-being, and legacy building.

Wisdom is not merely about knowing some answers to life's dilemmas. Wisdom is asking questions about old and new perspectives. A true wisdom search is weighted in discernment of what your experiences can teach you. Your wisdom journey also requires focus to not allow your senses to dull you, to rely on easy answers to complex problems, to allow others to make decisions for you, or to live by your assumptions or prejudices. Those who possess wisdom are not necessarily the hierarchical positioned, wealthy, or publicly lauded. Wisdom belongs to those who learn from life, no matter their station.

The path of wisdom is not without a starting point. This counsel of sages has a twofold charge: 1) accept responsibility for constructing a life of personal well-being and success, and 2) identify how you create well-being in your community. Only those who hear with their hearts and work diligently will find success in their journey.

In the wisdom search, ethical obedience is to be valued over intellectual development because ethics affect your decisions. If you choose to live ethically, you will naturally treat others with justice and fairness, speak truthfully and live responsibly with your family, neighbors and community. If you cultivate an ethical life-attitude, you will be trustworthy, while displaying integrity.

Life gives you daily opportunities to choose how to act. Choose wisely and decide responsibly in every situation. An ethical life is judged not by the words you say but by what you do.

Wisdom also calls you to do everything in moderation. Balance in life—particularly with food, drink, and the pursuit of wealth—is a consistent admonition of the wise. It is wise to be cautious at the table of a host, because excesses in these situations lead to perceptions about you that may not be true. Overindulgence of either food or drink may bring you dishonor, a questioning of your self-control, or speculation about your self-discipline.

Life is not a self-centered undertaking but rather a journey that brings well-being to society. If you are whole, then society can become complete through the combined responsibility we have for each other. In the end, planting seeds of wisdom teaches that your choices matter. Your actions have consequences, and your moral decisions, whether good or bad, reap their own rewards.

- Do you pay attention to the lessons presented in life, whether they happen to you or someone else?
- Do you make ethical and right decisions daily?
- Are you maintaining a balanced life as you pursue your work, learning, physical, family, spiritual or social needs?
- Are you living and acting responsibly in your workplace, family, and community?

SUMMER
S E A S O N

SUMMER IS THE SEASON FOR FIXING UP. We often spend them cleaning, repairing, and working on home projects that must be done before the hard blasts of winter winds. During these weeks, we turn our attention to tasks that require our energy and finances to improve or repair what might have been tattered over the colder winter season.

The Summer Season of leadership centers on principles that, when internally nurtured, produce the fruit of a successful life. During the Summer of their lives, leaders must focus on their attitudes about change, issues of integrity, how they sustain moral character, and live with balance. The Autumn and Winter of the year can bring harsh weather for leadership. If we have not readied ourselves during the Summer, we will become like the grasshopper, ill prepared for the darker times ahead.

This section is about nurturing core life principles. The readings and questions in this Season will ask you to consider your integrity, character, honesty and the legacy you are leaving behind. Through these pages, it is my hope that you will ask some of the most serious questions about who you are and what you will stand for in life and as a leader. If you do not become fit in this season, you may not be prepared for the many Seasons of Leadership.

RECOMMENDED BOOKS FOR THE SUMMER SEASON:

Leadership IS an Art. Max DePree. Dell Books: NY 1989

Leading Without Power: Finding Hope in Serving Community. Max DePree. Jossey-Bass Publishers: San Francisco 1997

If Aristotle Ran General Motors. Tom Morris. Henry Holt Publishers: NY 1997

Stewardship: Choosing Service Over Self-Interest. Peter Block. Berrett-Koehler: San Francisco 1993

Overcome Resistance to Change

The absurd man is he who never changes.

—Auguste Barthelemy
French journalist, poet &
political satirist
(1796-1867)

WE ARE CREATURES OF HABIT. We wear the same clothes, eat the same foods, and drive the same way to work every day of our lives. Changes in our routines are often unwelcome and even avoided at all costs.

Yet change may add new spice to life. Additionally, accepting change is a necessary component of your leadership journey. While the certainty of routine may give you a sense of stability, an unwillingness to change when times demand it can keep you from reaching your goals and dreams.

Just as the seasons change, you must change as well. From the time you are born, your cells change and multiply as you mature and grow through infancy and adolescence to adulthood. If your cells did not change, you would die. Leaders know that only movement forward to new opportunities brings life. To resist change could bring death.

Probably the most difficult places to change exist in our personal lives. Habits are hard to break. As we grow older, we often become entrenched in what is comfortable and easy to maintain. Changing your ways or habits is always a frontier ripe for adventure. The adventure of change may exist in a desire to quit unhealthy life styles, spend more time learning or change a personality quirk. But no matter the decision, it will require your energy and tenacity to make the transformation complete. The adventure of personal change may truly be one of the remaining frontiers for you.

• What areas of your life or leadership do you refuse to change? Why? What keeps you from seeing change as healthy and necessary for growth?

• What difference has this personal journey made in your life, leadership and opportunities?

The Permanence of Character

It is not what he has, or even what he
does which expresses the worth of a man,
but what he is.

—Henri Frederic Amiel
Swiss essayist, philosopher & poet
(1821-1881)

IN OUR CULTURE, THE PACKAGING IS KING. Marketers
and advertising agencies spend millions of dollars annually to
entice people to buy products they may not even need. The out-
ward packaging must be eye catching and alluring if you are to
spend your financial resources on a new or improved product.

People, too, spend millions of dollars to fashion a portrait
of themselves so that others gravitate to them. Through hous-
es, clothes, cars and a plethora of other possessions, they mold
an image that gives people an impression they are successful.

Yet by contrast, the truly successful person in life may
never possess any of the enticing packaging or material gains
of this world. A person is more than clothes or food, said
Jesus. They are what is on the inside.

One exposé caught my attention about Mother Theresa
as writers rushed to capture the vividness of her life when she

died. The article shared how Ivy League students packed an auditorium to hear this small, unassuming nun. What caught my attention was that the reporter related that many prominent people had graced this auditorium, but that no one could recall it ever being standing room only. Students absorbed with reverent silence and awe the words of a woman small in stature and plainly dressed, who came to this school without a large bank account or corporate title.

Horace Greeley, the newspaper man of the past century said, "Fame is a vapor; popularity is an accident; riches take wings. Only one thing endures and that is character." Effective leaders spend their lives cultivating a character of truth, integrity and nobleness. And whatever else comes their way is a bonus for being who they believe they are inside.

- Is your character more valuable to you than fame, popularity or riches? Why or why not?
- If you do not have character, what will you have in the long run?

Who Are You?

Gnothi seauton (Know Thyself).

—Inscription at the temple of
Apollo at Delphi, Classical Greek
location at Mt. Parnassus

DO YOU REALLY KNOW WHO YOU ARE? What
makes you tick? What are your motivations? How do you
perceive your world?

These questions are quickly answered by the inscription
at Delphi: "Know Thyself." But how do you really know
yourself? What methods lead you to a better understanding
of who you are?

Over the past decade, I have taken several personality
and learning tests that give me insight about who I am.
While they are not a panacea for every nuance of my life,
they do help me to know me.

I am an INTJ by the Myers-Briggs Type Indicator. These
letters mean I see my world as an introverted, intuitive,
thinking and judging person. While experts can tell a great
deal more about these types of personalities, let it suffice to
say I prefer logic, competence, problem solving, planning,
control and order in my life, work and play.

Also, I am a reflective learner, according to the 4MAT
Learning Style Indicator. This indicator tells me I like to

read, think and see information intuitively before I can give it a good response or opinion. People who know me realize they cannot spring a proposal on me at a meeting and ask me to approve it. I must have necessary time to review the contents, think about the wording and reflect on issues I might consider important but missing in the document.

Now, what does knowing myself in these ways have to do with anything? It is because of these two personality indicators that I now know why I am a habitual stacker of papers around my office and desk. While time management experts would tell me this does not make sense—since I prefer order and logic—I now realize stacking papers makes perfect sense to me. Let me explain.

Most productivity experts would say that filing papers brings efficiency and control over the flow of paper. But in my INTJness, I cannot touch, control or monitor the papers important to me if they are removed from my desk or floor. All the moving of dots, dashes, arrows, labels and filing papers out of sight to the time activated date is too much energy and not—in my mind—systematic. For me, taking the time to place all the arrows in the right sequence diverts my energy from thinking and acting on the material at hand. So as I experience being an INTJ, it is important for me to have papers in full view, lest I miss some important idea or interrelatedness that might exist from one paper to the next.

As a reflective learner, filing papers away or hiding them in electronic mediums prevents me from reflecting on them overall. Having papers out of my line of sight hinders me from seeing a thought here or a note there that all at once makes a connection, turning on the proverbial light of creativity or insight. For me, papers out of sight are truly out of mind.

Knowing myself in just this one way has made me realize that the time system used is less important than one's vision, discipline and persistence for accomplishing a task. The papers stacked around my office are beacons of proactivity—a visual reminder to keep moving toward my longed for vision and written goals. Through physically sorting and sifting, I remain connected—in a tangible way—with the tasks that are before me. Through the understanding of myself, I now have full confidence these paper mounds are lanterns of ideas, shedding light on my work, community and life goals. In my new-found awareness, I have concluded it is not the system you use, but how you use the system. I also am less stressed these days by not having an office that looks like someone else's space. Understanding why I stack is a fresh release.

Getting to know yourself can assist you in becoming more effective in all your work and life. It is also an adventure that will bring fresh perspectives to your relationships. Understanding why you do the things you do is a necessary part of becoming more human. Remember, however, knowing yourself is a freedom, but not an excuse to persist in ways detrimental to yourself or others.

• Take the Myers-Briggs Type Indicator and the 4MAT Learning Styles Indicator (by Bernice McCarthy). They are important tools for learning about yourself. You might also take the Minnesota Multiphasic Personality Inventory (MMPI) as a learning tool. But remember, take these inventories only with the help of a trained professional to assist you in interpreting the results.

Know the Cost of Living by Principle

> For which of you, desiring to build a
> tower, does not first sit down and count the
> cost, whether he has enough to complete it?
> Otherwise, when he has laid a foundation,
> and is not able to finish, all who see it begin
> to mock him saying, "This man began to
> build, and was not able to finish."
>
> —Jesus the Christ
> *The Bible*, Luke 14:28-29

BUILDING IS COSTLY. Architects, designers, contrac-
tors, and meeting after meeting all add to the cost of any project. Every cost aspect of building is detailed to give those
investing an idea about the return-on-investment, the risk to
capital investments and the consequences if planting commitments are not made or deadlines met.

As with building, principle, too, has a price. Integrity,
truth and character demand that we count the cost. Building
principle into our lives requires that we calculate the cost
before we find ourselves in the intensity of the fray. With no
inner foundation of commitment to principle, public displays

of character will fade in the heat of life's conflicts, as surely as grass will wither in a desert's sun.

Integrity, honesty, truth, justice—universally high standards—demand you live to their requirements, not compromising them to your needs. These principles do not change with time but remain beacons to which you are drawn. It is vital that you count the cost of following principle, lest you find yourself unable to fulfill the qualities that these virtues demand.

Principle that can withstand life's storms is constructed brick by brick. Living a life of principle means a willingness to stand firm in what is right even in the smallest of daily issues.

The cost of living up to the ultimate high call to principle may never happen to you. But because we live in a complex global society, you may be confronted by instances in which you must remain true to principle above all else. Living by principles may ask you to risk it all—your career, fortune, possessions, family, prestige—for the sake of what is right and true over what is expedient and easy.

Norman Augustine shares a story of cost about Ted Williams, the great Boston Red Sox hitter. After a disappointing season of batting under .300, Williams asked that his salary be cut by 25 percent because he wanted only what he deserved after a dismal year of baseball. Ted Williams had counted the cost of principle and made the appropriate decision, even in personal loss. You may never be asked to make such a sacrifice, but counting the cost of principle beforehand may indeed place you at the moment-of-truth when principle must win over personal gain.

William Wilhelm, in the book *Leaders of the Future*, invites you to consider the hard journey of leadership and principle when he writes:

> *Leaders have fewer degrees of behavioral freedom than those they are leading.*
> *Effective leadership requires a degree of control over libidinous impulses and some denial of personal gratification, which many*

> *people are unwilling to endure. This diminished personal freedom is a price for leadership. Those who are unwilling to pay it, however qualified they may be otherwise, are quickly denied the right to remain in their leadership role.*

Epictetus, a first century philosopher, gives us advice in counting the cost: "In every affair consider what precedes and follows, and then undertake it. Otherwise you will begin with spirit; but not having thought out the consequences, when some of them appear you will shamefully desist. Consider first what the matter is, and what your nature is able to bear."

The price of principle may never cost you personal loss. But principle may, at times, demand every cent you have invested. The lives of Nelson Mandela, Abraham Lincoln, Harriet Tubman, or Mahatma Gandhi let us know that imprisonment, perilous personal risk and even death may be the price tag of principle.

In his best selling book, *Strengthening Your Grip*, Charles Swindoll writes about costs, reminding us that the fight for principle—for truth, integrity and justice—can't be fought by "weary, ill-trained, noncommitted, half-hearted troops." The war of principle will be won in the long run by those who are willing to pay the price for principle, even if the cost is life itself. Counting the cost of principles and living them out must happen in every waking moment. Living by principle is not a once-in-a-while venture, but an all-the-time choice.

• Are the principles of integrity, truth, honesty, or justice so important to you that you would choose to live them out rather than to not live by their standards?

• Are there areas of your life that you have compromised? Are you willing to make the needed corrections to come under the calling of principle?

• When confronted by a situation of principle, do you weigh your actions before making a move?

Talk is Cheap

There is plenty of courage among us for
the abstract but not for the concrete.

—Helen Keller
American author
(1880-1968)

THE TALK SHOWS THAT SPEND HOURS DEBATING
current issues are intriguing to me. For hour upon hour, the
hosts banter back and forth with guests about this dilemma
or that tragedy. The humor of all the heated discussion and
display of emotion to me is the dilemma is still going on
while the participants appear on another show to debate
another life scenario.

The sadness of all this abstract debate is that the same
emotion and rhetoric are evident in the workplace, classrooms
or social settings. There seems to be, as Keller observed, a
great amount of courage for defending or bashing ideas in the
abstract. The real test of our courage is in tackling the concrete, in doing something to change the situation.

We admire those that seem to go the extra mile. Jimmy
and Rosalyn Carter through Habitat for Humanity, Mother
Theresa in Calcutta, or even children handing out blankets
to the homeless have found there is no cure in debate. The

remedy for dilemmas and tragedies in this world is in the courage and humility to stop talking and start doing.

- What issues do you love to passionately debate? Make a list. Next to that list, make notes of what you have personally done to make changes or correct those issues?
- What are the issues you love to debate in your workplace? Make a list. Next to those items, make notes on what you are personally doing to stop these issues from happening or how you are finding ways to turn them into positive situations.

Accept Accountability

Today responsibility is often meant to denote duty, something imposed upon one another from the outside. But responsibility, in its true sense, is an entirely voluntary act; it is my response to the needs, expressed or unexpressed, of another human being.

—Erich Fromm
German-born social psychoanalyst
(1900-1980)

IT IS OUR DUTY AND RESPONSIBILITY to evaluate those we supervise in the workplace. That right has been the supervisor's since the science of management crawled out of its infancy. How else will supervisors know whether the organization is running efficiently and effectively unless they evaluate employees? But what would happen if those you supervise had the opportunity to evaluate you?

I have asked those I supervise to evaluate my personal performance as I interact with them. I have been doing this over the past five years of my career. This evaluation is a necessary part of my growth as a person and leader. Their feedback helps me to recognize the areas of my own style that are creating barriers to their work.

You risk damaging your ego when you ask for such feedback. At times, this tool can be hurtful. But while the results may hurt, like medicine, they will only make you better over time.

The following are some of the questions I ask my staff:

- Do I listen to your needs?
- Do I stay informed of new concepts and ideas?
- Am I willing to challenge the status quo?
- Am I honest in my dealings with your area?
- Do I follow through on requests made by you or others in your area?
- Do I seem interested in your personal welfare?

Effective leaders make themselves accountable to others. Through such questions and feedback, others help the leader become better as an employee and as a human being. Your challenge is to develop tools, such as this one, that will be agreements of accountability between you and those around you.

- Are you willing to be vulnerable to those you lead through a written feedback method?
- Once you have the feedback, are you willing to change who you are in order to become a better leader and person?

On the following page is an actual copy of the evaluation form I use with my staff.

PERFORMANCE EVALUATION FORM

Working in a specific area over a period of time without evaluating one's performance can narrow the focus of activities and effectiveness of that person. It is also important to look for areas that need improvement in relationships and work assignments. Please take a few minutes to evaluate my performance in working with you and your department. Be as candid as you wish.

David Neidert . . . (Circle only one response per question)

EXCELLENT = 5   POOR = 1

• listens to my needs	5 4 3 2 1
• is available to me for questions or concerns	5 4 3 2 1
• stays informed of new concepts and ideas	5 4 3 2 1
• is willing to challenge the status quo	5 4 3 2 1
• is honest in his dealings with my area	5 4 3 2 1
• supports my interests to upper level management	5 4 3 2 1
• allows me to run my operation as I understand my duties and assignment	5 4 3 2 1
• is open to dialogue when there is a conflict	5 4 3 2 1
• models the best of our division and its goals	5 4 3 2 1
• follows through on requests made by me and others in my area	5 4 3 2 1
• provides guidance as needed for my area of responsibility	5 4 3 2 1
• has a clear and hopeful vision for our division	5 4 3 2 1

- seems interested in my personal welfare   5 4 3 2 1

- recognizes me and others when we
  achieve our goals and aspirations   5 4 3 2 1

- provides clear instructions for
  assignments given to me   5 4 3 2 1

- promotes an open door policy and
  open communication   5 4 3 2 1

- provides supervision I believe is
  adequate to perform my duties   5 4 3 2 1

- maintains confidentiality   5 4 3 2 1

- encourages me to grow in my profession   5 4 3 2 1

- holds me accountable for tasks
  assigned to me   5 4 3 2 1

PLEASE COMPLETE THE FOLLOWING:

What does David Neidert do that helps and supports me the most?

What would you like David Neidert to either stop doing or do differently?

What would you like David Neidert to start doing?

Practice Makes Permanent

Nothing is more powerful than habit.

—Ovid
Roman poet, from Ars amatoria
(43 BC-AD 18)

THE **GREAT DANGER** in starting a leadership journey is that you can become complacent with what you know at any given point. There is also a danger in any leadership study to make it a cerebral pursuit. Our problems quickly surface when we are in stressful circumstances that interfere with what is being learned, forcing us to rely on habit. When trials drain your energy, it is easy to forget all you have learned and revert to what you instinctually remember.

Fully experiencing and practicing the best of leadership is vital to your long-term effectiveness. It is one thing to learn leadership through self-help books and one-day seminars, yet quite another to live their teachings. You must realize that in times of stress or obstacles, your habits will win over principle. Learning must be coupled with constant practice if leadership lessons are to win over habit.

The adage "You reap what you sow" takes on enormous significance in the application of leadership knowledge over habit. What you are learning about leadership will not be useful if you do not nurture what you are learning through frequent practice. Just as you cannot do simple arithmetic without practice, neither can you expect to be an effective leader without practicing leadership. You've often heard that practice makes perfect—it also makes permanent.

- It is most comfortable for us to continue to use what works for us. Take time to reflect on what you normally do in a stressful situation. Make an effort to recognize this and how effective you are as a result of how you respond.
- Are you daily practicing the characteristics of leadership? If not, why do you continue to put off assimilating these effective elements into your actions? How would your daily behavior change if you practiced what you are learning?

Make Room
for Solitude

What a commentary on our civilization,
when being alone is considered suspect;
when one has to apologize for it, make
excuses, hide the fact that one practices it—
like a secret vice!

—Anne Morrow Lindbergh
American poet & essayist

I **HIT THE ALARM CLOCK BUTTON** nearly every morning at 5:30 am. After a quick shower and shave, I settle onto
the sofa for a time of quiet reflection and prayer. It is an
important thirty minutes for me as I reflect on the day, think
about my friends and family and ask God for wisdom to live
rightly and purposefully in the waking hours ahead.

Taking time to center and focus on your day and purpose is
essential for a healthy and balanced life. Many of the great spiritual leaders of all ages demonstrated that solitude and reflection are necessary ingredients for living well. The world is too
much with us, and it is in solitude that we allow ourselves to
regain the spiritual strength for the stresses we encounter.

Time for daily spiritual renewal does not have to be complicated. In the first minutes of my own meditation, I thank

God for just being alive one more day to complete my purpose. I also express my gratitude for family and friends, what I possess and the journey I have already experienced.

Next, I focus on concerns for family and friends and situations that will require my deepest patience, attention and strength. I almost always end my time alone the same way with the words, "God, give me wisdom for this day to be all I am meant to be."

The time alone in solitude passes rapidly for me. But I emerge fresh and ready from that one-half hour to face all that will come my way. As I rise from that sofa, I always feel quieted and calm. And the side benefit of this time alone is that it prepares in me a grateful spirit for all I will encounter throughout the day.

Find a place for your solitude. A simple chair in the stillness of a morning provides a place for deep spiritual renewal and rest from this harried world.

• Try rising one-half hour earlier every morning to spend time in prayer, reflection or meditation. After one week ask, "How do I feel throughout a day after starting my mornings in solitude?"

• Do you believe there is benefit for personal spiritual renewal or is that only for other people? Why do you hold that perception?

Control What
You Say

Consider that a great forest is set on fire by a small spark. The tongue is also a fire . . . Out of the same mouth come blessings and curses. This should not be so.

—James, brother of Jesus
The Bible, Epistle of James 3:1-12

YOUR TONGUE IS AN INTERESTING MUSCLE. It is a tool that can bring great praise, but also abounding pain. The adage "Sticks and stones may break my bones, but words can never harm me" is nonsense. Words spoken in anger, or gossip flippantly repeated, cut the very heart of people, sometimes wounding them for life.

Leaders work diligently to tame their tongue. They strive endlessly not to partake in gossip, rumors, or discussions that might wound or injure another human being. Through self discipline and control, they make their tongues instruments of praise and encouragement. With their lips they bring dignity, respect and healing into the lives of others.

Your tongue is a small muscle. In and of itself it has no ability to do anything. But your tongue is attached directly to your heart. If your heart is deceitful, then it will move your tongue to slick and fancy maneuvers of the truth. And if your heart is filled with respect and dignity for others, it will release encouragement or shut down completely to avoid hurting someone.

The spoken word has a magical and elusive quality. Once those air waves leave your mouth, they cannot be captured in a net or jerked back to your throat. Words contain the power for setting the heart ablaze—either for good or destruction, for praise or ridicule, for truth or deceit. Your tongue discloses what lies inside your heart. It is critical you tend to that conduit.

- Do you regularly participate in gossip or sharing rumors about others? Why?
- What will you do this week to "tame your tongue" and make it a blessing, not a curse?

Listen to Your Body Talk

If one had to name a single, all-purpose instrument of leadership, it would be communication.

—John W. Gardner
Educator & leadership author

YOUR WAKING HOURS ARE LITERALLY SATURATED with communication. It appears that information is being endlessly transmitted, whether through the morning news, telephone conversations, dancing computer screens or ceaseless streams of memos.

Leaders take communication seriously. Many leadership scholars advocate speech lessons and presentation skills for those desiring to share vital messages of vision and purpose to those within their influence. Effective leaders spend the necessary time and effort honing skills of language and the written word. Who has not been stirred by an eloquent speech, a deeply inspiring sermon or a captivating vision woven through linguistic clarity?

Yet for all the writing and talking, speech classes and seminars on presentation skills, it is astonishing to realize that a mere 7-10% of our normal day is verbal. An enormous majority of what we say is communicated through nonverbal queues, like your face, body posture, or the use of your time. From childhood, we learn to trust the nonverbal signs we encounter above the spoken word. We quickly learn that nonverbal queues negate the greatest attempts at oration by parents, those in authority or our leaders. We learn to trust our nonverbal instincts regarding action over rhetoric almost before we know we are alive.

If you believe this is a rather naïve observation, recall a time when you walked into a room and someone asked, "Having a bad day?" While you simply walked into the room—probably making no guttural noises—your body sent a volume of meaning to the person asking the question. Or consider a conversation you had with someone, only to walk away remarking to yourself, "That's nonsense." How do you know? What made you trust your gut over their words? It is no wonder that the communication expert, Ray Birdwhitsell, observed as humans we are multi-sensoral, who occasionally verbalize.

One evening when our children were older, my wife and I returned home from dinner and a movie. As we entered the door, our son was moving around the family room in a rather stiff and awkward manner. Immediately we asked him what had happened. David gave the genetically inborn response handed down from Adam and Eve, "Oh, nothing." But his demeanor told us something was amiss. So we asked one more time. That second question was enough to break his defenses and he told us how his sister had pierced her nose! As parents, we knew immediately something was amiss from the behavior of our son. It is through experience that non-verbal queues tell us volumes about what is unspoken. (As a side bar, we have learned these acts of bodily perforation are often a phase. My wife and I have learned hair color will always grow out and pierced places will always grow shut—with time. Be patient).

We communicate daily through our behavior and actions. Nonverbal language is an outgrowth of our character and leadership beliefs. In minute ways, we lay bare our natures, whether it is in the arrangement of our offices, a raised eyebrow or the tone and quality of our voices. Effective leaders are conscious of their actions. They also work diligently to match their words with their deeds.

If leaders desire to unleash the power in people, they will work tirelessly at making their words and actions consistent. Inconsistency between language and action will cancel out what is said, no matter how often, loudly, eloquently or clearly spoken. If your speech does not match your behavior, those within your sphere of influence will, over time, begin to discount what you say in favor of what you don't say.

Grade yourself against these observations regarding action over words. They may seem trivial, but they reveal inconsistencies that will require your attention.

• Do you complain about subordinates taking breaks and lunches that are too long because punctuality is important, yet you arrive ten to fifteen minutes late or leave early?

• Are you pushing people to stay cutting edge in their fields through memos and speeches, but you have not attended a seminar in years or spent money to acquire educational opportunities for those you supervise?

• Are your speeches filled with the challenge for greater customer service, yet when a customer gets to your office, there is no time for them, or the tone of your voice and body language let them know they are a bother, not an opportunity?

• You have stated publicly that certain events sponsored by your organization are critical for growth, yet you miss them regularly due to "scheduling conflicts?"

• When a person you supervise comes to see you, do they wait for long periods of time, yet when you appear in their work area you expect immediate attention from them?

• Is the work you perform more important than the assignments given to others you supervise, and do you expect them to do your requests first, even if they have work needed by a larger group of clients?

- Do you wholeheartedly agree to a structure or format for work flow and efficiency because it is good for the organization, but when the structure hits your department, you resist with boisterous defense and a defiant attitude?

Remember the Golden Rule

Do unto others as you would have them do to you. For this is the sum of the law and the prophets.

—Jesus the Christ
The Bible, Matthew 7:12

TODAY, PLATINUM IS IN. Whether it is the premier level of a credit card or the grand distinction in the music industry, platinum seems to say it all. Platinum is also equated with the epitome of relationships as reflected in the phrase, "Treat others the way they want to be treated."

While it may sound simple to treat others the way they prefer, there are many problems in bringing those wishes to reality. Treating others how they want to be treated keeps us guessing about others' wants or needs. Being a mind reader is no easy task, yet going platinum may thrust you into that vocation. Trying to treat others from their perspective may also cause you relational errors because of your not understanding ethnic background or personal history. Ultimately, you may never find yourself adequate in meeting others' wishes because they may not know what they truly need. Going platinum sounds great, but in human relationships, gold still glitters.

The Golden Rule makes revolutionary sense today as it has for the past two millennia. This relationship measurement makes sense simply because it takes you to the deepest recesses of how you want to be treated as a human being. If you strip away the veneer of superficial personal wants, you encounter the human elements about yourself. On the surface, you may want various earthly creature comforts. Yet by systematically and continually scraping away the layers of fleshly wants, you will discover a foundation of what all people truly covet as human beings.

When you ask reflective questions about yourself, surroundings or purposes in life, you gradually move toward personal success through self-awareness. Contemplating the meaning of the Golden Rule opens your own self-awareness for relating equitably and justly toward others. Searching for the highest good in human nature reveals not only your desired treatment, but makes you sensitive to the treatment sought by others.

Reflecting and contemplating on how you would like to be treated, at your deepest human level, sets the parameters for doing or acting toward others. As I think about human dignity, it is easy for me to list how I want to be treated because I know those traits intimately.

I desire to be treated with care, kindness, respect, fairness, truthfulness, honesty, justice, and sincerity. I desire others to listen to my ideas, emotions, and dreams. I want people to know me before they make judgments about me from my physical form. I do not want people to provoke or antagonize me. I want others to promote and acknowledge me by my merit and not my appearance. I desire for others to value me as a person for my talents and gifts. I hope others will never consider acting in a way that would wrong or harm me. I feel valued when others show self-control and accountability in their relationships with me. I want others to expect the best from me, whether it is at work or play. I desire for people to cry with me when I am alone or suffering. I hope others will be merciful toward me when I make mistakes or fail. I need encouragement and optimism when all seems lost. I desire to belong and be included. I enjoy people who are genuine in their personality and dealings with me. And ultimately, I desire to be loved.

Is this not also how you would like to be treated? "The Golden Rule," writes Tom Morris, "directs me to use my imagination in such a way as to create empathy for others." Living the Golden Rule will require your imagination and your energy. In the end, the Golden Rule is the sum total of all the leadership books on this planet.

What are the things you would like people to do to you? Would you like them to listen, give respect, care, treat you fairly, or love you? In your thinking, try to get beyond superficial desires like money or status. Make the most exhaustive list you can of the ways you would like others to treat you when you consider your deepest human nature and human needs. Now, do them to others!

Leadership: Empowering Others

The glory that goes with wealth and beauty is fleeting and fragile; virtue is a possession glorious and eternal.

—Sallust
Roman senator and historian
(86 BC- 34 BC)

FOR CENTURIES, PEOPLE HAVE TRIED to understand the character elements of effective leadership. But just when it seems the golden fleece is found, a new set of questions emerges.

And yet, we should still seek answers about the nature of leadership because in doing so we reflect not only on work but also on purpose.

The philosopher Aristotle reasoned that living with a purpose brings us ultimately to happiness. This purposeful living was more than achieving the creature comforts and collecting assets. To live with purpose rests upon the examination of one's life, so that in the end a person may live as fully as possible.

Great leadership is about moral character and living to the most excellent qualities valued in the human experience. Leaders are expected to guide those around them in examining their lives, in finding fulfillment, in answering the question, "Am I fulfilling my meaning through my life and work?" The leader is essential as people seek to make sense of their lives and the purpose for engaging in work.

Although Aristotle constructed a framework of what people should expect from others, his reasoning may also be applied to leaders. The expectations we should have of each other for the common good are few, but they are powerful if lived.

First, Aristotle believed people should have a vision and mission. A leader's purposeful reflection and action in setting the vision are critical for the climate and direction of those around them. Beyond this task, leaders seek ways to challenge people to construct their own personal mission—one that reflects not only their relationships to their organization but also their connection with families and communities.

Second, Aristotle implored us to think. A leaders asks "Why?" and also gives quality thinking to clarify the issues. Leaders must be reflective in their thinking, seeking wisdom as they consider what is best for the enterprise. Learning and careful reflection must be modeled by leaders, so that the urgencies of the moment do not sidetrack the principles of long-term health.

Aristotle also observed that keeping promises and telling the truth are critical in all relationships. We have a duty to keep our promises and tell the truth. Keeping your promises means people can rely on you to do what you say. Trust is built on commitment to goals and consistent behavior in carrying them out. Truthfulness and credibility do not come from words but spring from consistent action and reliability of behavior. Effective leaders do as they intend.

Mutual accountability is a two-way street between follower and leader. Leaders share their personal performance goals with the entire entity, and they acknowledge where they are not meeting their goals. Trust emerges from this display of humanness and action rooted in commitment to personal performance.

Finally, Aristotle believed we must expect financial health and solvency from each other. Leaders know that debt restricts people, saps productivity and energy, and may force institutions to compromise standards of excellence in serving their constituents. Staying financially solvent is among the priorities that leaders have on the agenda, as they seek to balance money and assets with people and relationships.

The bottom line of leadership is to create an empowering climate where people find energy, adequate resources and a control of their own destiny. Aristotle's ultimate reasoning about virtuous living is that our personal lives, in these ways, do influence the good of all society.

• Do you challenge others to develop their own mission in life? Do you use every opportunity afforded to you to express your own mission?

• Are you disciplined in setting aside time to reflect on your leadership and life mission?

• Do you keep your promises?

• Do you believe you are accountable to those around you for your actions and the results of your behavior?

• Are you prudent with your personal finances and the finances of others entrusted to you?

Stand in the Light

BUYING SOME MERCHANDISE in fluorescent light is risky. It may look just fine when it is in the glow of these burning tubes. Yet when you get that item into daylight, it takes on a whole new appearance. It may even be that in sunlight, the flaws or true colors will be revealed.

Honest people do not fear the fluorescent light or the contrasting brightness of sunlight. They are the same in both lights. They are what you see. Honest people live openly in the public and private areas of their lives. They do not act in the darkness in ways that would be unbearable to acknowledge in the sunlight.

The Gospel of John records a poignant story of the dishonesty at work in us. Teachers of the law caught a woman in adultery. They put her in the center of a crowd and challenged Jesus, "This woman was caught in the act of adultery and by our laws should be put to death by stoning. What do you say?" In a calm, but authoritative voice Jesus responded, "If any one of you is without sin, be the first one to throw a stone at her." One by one, from the oldest first to the youngest, the crowd dispersed, leaving Jesus standing alone with the woman. In their hearts, they knew that their own acts in the darkness would bring them into the center of the crowd if they, too, had been found out.

Albert Schweitzer observed, "Truth has no special time of its own. Its hour is always—now." Being honest is not for whispering in the darkness or just shouting from the rooftops. Honesty's hour is always now.

It would be an understatement to say my daughter and I have not always agreed. During her adolescent years, we often found ourselves at polar extremes of ideas, attitudes, moral values and behaviors that were acceptable in our home. To my heartache, I must confess at times harsh words opened a relational chasm between us.

But while I tried to be accommodating to her growth, I verbally committed to her I would never compromise my values or character in our struggles. They were not negotiable. I vowed I would continue to speak honestly about the prevailing attitudes from the perspective I believed was principled and right. And whether she liked it or not, the boundaries set would come from those principles, no matter how restrictive or severe they appeared.

Now in her twenties, my daughter and I have renewed belief and love for each other. One evening during a conversation, she caught me off guard by saying, "Dad, you are the most honest person I know in my life." In a twinkling, I was humbled to know through all our opposition and heartache I had been consistently who I thought I was inside.

A leader worth our allegiance knows a congruent character is not optional. They know leadership extracts a price for principle, and they are willing to pay it. In its simplest terms, transformational leaders affirm and follow Jesus' instruction, "Let your yes be yes and your no be no."

- Are you honest in all matters and dealings with people or possessions? Why or why not? What keeps you from being honest in all situations?
- If someone gave you too much change at a restaurant or did not charge you for an item at the grocery store, would you tell them and pay what is due? Why or why not?
- Are your actions in private able to bear the light of public scrutiny?
- What are the areas of inconsistency in your life? How will you change them into places of consistency between words and deeds? How will you develop integrity between what you say and who you are?

Live Seamlessly

Who we are is what we do in private.

—Dwight L. Moody
U.S. evangelist & religious writer
(1837-1899)

"IF YOU CAN BE TRUSTED, whether alone or in a crowd . . . if you are truly a person of your word and convictions, you are fast becoming an extinct species." In today's open air market of values, Charles Swindoll seems to make an accurate observation of the times.

Leaders live with a deep sense of integrity. Integrity is the personal code that leaders have incorporated into who they are and how they act. Integrity is not a once in a while behavior but an all of the time decision to live not only by the law, but with the intent of the law.

In a day of situational ethics and values lived in relationship to perceived constitutionally guaranteed beliefs, it is distressing to think about a defining and limiting word like integrity. Integrity means a wholeness, an entirety, an uprightness of a person. A word originating from the garment industry, it literally means to be seamless, as a garment woven into one piece. Living with integrity is to behave in a whole way, not acting in an inconsistent or incongruent manner from your words or beliefs.

The matching of your actions with your words is the spirit of integrity. Being a person of integrity is a conscious, daily checking and rechecking of your behaviors against what you say publicly. The peril awaiting any leader, organization or community is when their private lives and public promises are in contradiction.

You must remind yourself daily that people are watching you. You must also consider that people are not always waiting for the momentous events of your life to prove your integrity. They are watching the little, almost undetectable actions that over time reveal your true nature. The seeds of integrity are intricately imbedded in the Law of the Farm, that is, planting now—at this very moment—to ensure a harvest that will sustain you in the years ahead. Planting integrity demands you sow in the smallest of ways every day, not waiting for some spectacle of public forum to display your fruits.

At the very soul of integrity is your choice to live privately as if you were in the full gaze of others. Ultimately having integrity as a leader and person may be the most precious attribute nurtured throughout your life.

AN IQ TEST (INTEGRITY QUOTIENT):

- Do you drive the speed limit, not only when your family is in the car or a police officer is behind you, but when you are alone?
- Do you report all your income on your taxes?
- If a clerk at a store gives you too much change, do you put it in your pocket or return the amount over what is due to you?
- When your supervisor is away from the work site, do you play or work as hard as if he or she were there?
- Do you fudge on expense accounts from your employer?
- Do you spend just five extra minutes on a break, when you should have returned to work?
- If you allowed others to scrutinize your personal work, would they find you hard working, productive and dedicated or lazy and half-committed?

- When in a conversation, are you duplicitous—saying one thing to those within earshot and quite another when you are in the company of others?
- Do you keep your promises?
- Are you willing to admit when you have done something that does not have integrity in it—even publicly?

Lead with Mercy

Cowards are cruel, but the brave love
mercy and delight to save.

—John Gay
English playwright and poet
(1685-1732)

LIVING BY THE PRINCIPLE OF THE LEX TELIONIS—an
eye for an eye—is in abundance today. In your face, it's my
space attitudes plant an anger that sees fruition in abuse, vio-
lence and retaliation. Talking about mercy has no place in a
society that persists in making sure 'no one messes with me.'

Mercy means you are willing to extend kindness or
clemency to others instead of strictness or severity, even
though deserved. Mercy is persistent and courageous in making
relationships work, even when it would be easier to let them go
in times of difficulty or stress. In mercy there is genuine compassion for others, a willingness to see with the eyes of respect
and to value people just because they are human beings.

Probably the greatest example of mercy is captured in
the parable of the Good Samaritan. During a journey, a man
was attacked, robbed, beaten and left to die. On two occasions, two different men passed by him as he lay dying. Both
saw his condition and need for attention, but their own
agendas, safety, and attitude toward this stranger were para-

173

mount in not helping him. It may also be these two men thought he had it coming to him for being in this place at the wrong time of day. But no matter what the circumstances, they ignored him and went on their way.

But one man did stop when he saw the life ebbing away from another human being. Out of compassion and mercy for a fellow traveler, he interrupted his own journey, his own agenda, and risked his own safety to help a person in distress. This man even spent his own money for the injured traveler and agreed to pay his hospital stay when he returned to the area. It was this man, as the parable shares, that displayed mercy. Out of respect for another human being, he involved himself for the well-being and wholeness of another traveler.

Holding an attitude of mercy creates a healthy involvement in the lives of other people. Those who are merciful echo with Dickens his words from *A Christmas Carol*, "Humanity is my business." Mercy is a gift we choose to give out of care for others. We are neither obligated nor forced to display mercy. It is rather a freewill offering of ourselves to bring prosperity and wholeness instead of harm and retaliation.

Mercy not only affects the receiver, but it also changes the one granting mercy. Shakespeare wrote, "The quality of mercy is twice blessed. It blesses him that gives and him that takes." While it is easier to mete out an eye for an eye, it is more life-transforming to choose an action of forbearance.

- When a person affronts you, do you jump to the lex telionis? Why or why not?
- Do you consider mercy a display of weakness? Why or why not?
- Have you ever responded in mercy to another? What happened to them? To you?

Give Something Extra

*And if someone wants to sue you and
take your tunic, let him have your cloak as
well. Likewise if a person in power calls you
to go one mile with them, instead go two.*

—Jesus the Christ
The Bible, Matthew 5:40

WHAT A PREPOSTEROUS SUGGESTION! How dare
Jesus expound this teaching about relationships. How unreal-
istic and unreasonable to give something extra, when the
other person has no right to ask for it. Besides, it's ours anyway.

The Cajun culture leads us to consider planting a seed of
extra giving. The essence of this lifestyle is nestled in the
lagniappe. The lagniappe is a wonderful and risky life choice
that we often forget. The lagniappe is literally giving a little
something extra, providing the baker's dozen or going the
second mile. Giving something extra is important for our
society, particularly in a time when many seek self-gratifica-
tion above other's needs. You might ultimately create an attitude of giving in others by living as examples of the
lagniappe. Living by the principle of the lagniappe is a powerful lifestyle uncommon for our time.

We are witnessing a rebirth of this Cajun principle through random acts of kindness. Acts like these are the very essence of this principle. Doing something extra—particularly if it is done in secret or without public fanfare—awakens our spirit to the attitude of giving.

Living the lagniappe slowly changes relationships. Yet more important, that spirit of giving, consciously chosen, begins to change us.

• Would you be willing to give up something or go the extra mile, or do you believe there is no such thing as a free lunch?

• Write down just one lagniappe activity you will perform today. And after today, decide what you will do tomorrow. These constant acts will ultimately become habits that will ultimately change you.

Use Time Wisely—
It's Your Life

*Those who make the worst use of their
time are the first to complain of its brevity.*

—Jean de La Bruyere
French satirist
(1645-1696)

JUST IMAGINE YOUR BANK ACCOUNT receives $86,400
every morning. Nice! You can use it in any way you want with
no strings attached . . . except two: you cannot carry the balance forward to tomorrow, and the account zeros out at mid-
night. Otherwise you are free to use the money at will.

In reality, you do have such an account, according to
Brian Tracy. It is called time. At the start of every day, you
have a time account of 86,400 seconds to use as you want.
But at the end of the day, it zeros out. What you have not
used or have used improperly is gone, never to be recovered
again. So believe it or not, think about it or not, live it or
not, you have all the time there is to do all the things you
desire. It is unfortunate that we live in a society that constantly bemoans, "There is never enough time!" But the fact
is, you have all the time there is—86,400 seconds every day.

I have used four different time management systems in the past twenty years. I even created my own hybrid system to meet my particular learning style. All time systems have their strengths and weaknesses. But the one poignant point I learned through them all is the system does not make you effective, it is the time choices you make that enhance your productivity.

We often rely on time systems to keep us on track. But our problem is we have not learned to make choices with the gray areas of our time. Planners keep us on track for meetings or completing deadlines, but they do not manage the time between the time. It is here we often equate busyness with productivity. Yet some of the most productive time will be sitting still and thinking through an idea or project before you start shuffling papers. You must realize that the open time slots on your planner are actually more important than what you schedule.

Effective leaders know the value of time. The use of time is within their control. They constantly acknowledge the important life matters that quietly wait for their attention. They do not allow themselves to be seduced by time wasters or unimportant matters. Leaders work on important activities such as goal setting, preparation, reading, creating opportunities and living a balanced life. They also intently work on the gray areas of time that rapidly slip away.

If you desire to leave a leadership and life legacy, you must separate from the bemoaning crowd. Using your time wisely is a daily choice. The question is, "What decisions will you make about spending your time account?"

The following are some principles for mastering your use of time. Again, they will only help if you make daily choices about the seconds available to you.

• *Set priorities for your work.* What must you accomplish today to move you closer to your mission and goals?

• *Set weekly goals.* Break down your mission into manageable pieces of time. Work on them consistently by setting appointments with yourself—on your calendar—to work on those specific items.

• *Beware of procrastination.* Procrastination will keep you from getting to the results you want.

• *Watch rationalizing your situation.* Rationalizing your situation or why you cannot meet your mission will become the reality. Rationalization focuses on how others will take care of you instead of how you will take care of yourself.

• *Distinguish between urgent and unimportant activities.* Not urgent and not important activities are busywork without a goal, just hanging out, or escape activities like hours of television. Not urgent but important activities are reading, planning, preparation, goal setting, relationship building, etc. This second group will move you toward your mission and goals.

• *Learn to say "NO."* When you have too much to accomplish or too many activities, you risk going off track from your mission or goals.

• *Keep your promises to yourself.* Separate what you should do and could do from what you will do. Much of our stress comes not from what we should or could do, but from not keeping our promises to ourselves for what we agreed to do. If it takes less than two minutes to do it, do it now. This will give you a sense of accomplishment and not allow you to pile unmet expectations—unmet agreements—on yourself.

• *Get up earlier or stay up later.* Which one you choose will depend on your natural body clock, but you can gain a tremendous amount of time by just adding ½ hour to either side of your day.

• *Use the cassette player in your car for learning.* Instead of always listening to the radio, use commuting time to sharpen your mind. Today, many books come on audio tape.

The list is almost endless. Discover what you are doing that wastes time, and make the changes in your life that will lead to more effective use of your time.

• Stephen Covey asks an important question, "What one thing are you currently not doing, that if you did on a regular basis, would make a positive difference in your life?" Identify this one thing (maybe two or three), and put them on your calendar. Keep track of what difference doing them makes in your life.

Are You Happy?

The happy man is not he who seems thus
to others, but who seems thus to himself.

—Publilius Syrus
Latin mime & actor
(1st century BC)

MY DAUGHTER HAD JUST TALKED to the young man a few days earlier. The brother of her high school friend, he seemed happy and content with life. What a tragedy, then, to find one morning on the front page of our newspaper the story of his attempted murder-suicide. In a moment of anger, he had taken his own life.

Appearances of happiness are all around us. We see individuals and couples where all looks "happy" only to hear of a personal tragedy or a broken relationship. Happiness is not what others see, but how we see our personal life circumstances.

Comparing ourselves to others seems to breed dissatisfaction with our life. Happiness is rooted in a willingness to be satisfied with your own progress, reaching your own goals and living as you believe you are intended. Discontent and unhappiness are quickly upon you when you lose sight of your dreams and begin focusing on what someone else possesses. The truth is there will always be others who have more or less than you possess—a bigger house, finer clothes, a fatter bank account, a higher paying job or public recognition. Your challenge is to remain focused on what brings satisfaction to you as you measure yourself against your own dreams. Happiness in life will come when you learn to be content in whatever circumstances you encounter.

Interestingly, happiness is not found when searching for it. Searching for happiness alone, said social philosopher Eric Hoffer, is our greatest cause of unhappiness. Happiness comes as a by-product of living purposefully, working hard and believing you are making a contribution to others. When we are cutting paths that bring us to our goals and dreams, we will be amazed that our companion along the way is happiness.

• When you consider your life right now, are you happy? Why or why not?

• What do you believe will bring you happiness, joy and contentment in the years ahead?

• Do you spend energy comparing yourself and what you possess against other's fortunes? Does this bring you peace or anxiety?

Amidst the Work, Don't Forget Your Personal Relationships

Few people do business well who do nothing else.

—Lord Chesterfield
(Philip Dormer Stanhope)
English politician and wit
(1694-1773)

THE ADAGE, ALL WORK AND NO PLAY makes Jack a dull boy, is a critical testament for effective leadership and life legacy. It is easy in our culture to get sidetracked into believing that we are only meant for work. It seems strange that in a society with so many recreational opportunities we have a growing number of people who consider themselves workaholics.

There is a heavy price that will be extracted in your personal development, particularly if you develop in a vacuum. Often planting and tending to the goals and vision for our lives takes so much energy that we forget that it is all for

183

naught if we come to the end with no meaningful human relationships. It is critical and essential to your well-being that, during the journey of self-development, you plant and nurture balanced relationships. Successes may be clouded or without legacy if you are intently bent on individualism while intentionally or unknowingly choking out relationships that make us human. In the work to grow individually and in your career, you must not forget you were made for other human beings.

Effective leaders understand the fragile balance among the components of their lives. If you are to live with legacy, you must balance your work, physical, social, spiritual, and family needs. Getting out of kilter can throw you off course, ultimately forcing you to miss the very things in life that make for success—and happiness.

Jesus asks an important question in the Gospel of Matthew. Of all humanity he inquires, "What good will it be for a person if they gain the whole world, yet forfeit their soul?" Unbalanced and unbridled self-development or career activities can exact an oppressive price.

Your funeral will be what you make of it. The words spoken there will depend on what you have done in the waking moments of your life. You can choose what is said. Do you prefer, "They were a good friend, lover, and role model for others." Or would you prefer, "They worked 90 hours a week." You make the choice daily.

• Are you living a balanced life among the areas of your work, physical, social, spiritual and family needs? If not, why? If work is dominating all your time, what are you sacrificing in the rest of your life?

• When you become aware that you are out of balance with relationships, do you make an apology to significant people in your life for your actions?

• When you are with people you value relationally, are you present with them or preoccupied with your own self-interests?

• Do you set aside uninterrupted quality time for developing relationships with your family, friends, and others significant to you?

Retain a Youthful Vitality

Youth is a quality, not a matter of circumstance.

—Frank Lloyd Wright
American architect
(1867-1959)

I HAVE MET THEM AND SO HAVE YOU. People in their 20s, 30s, 40s and 50s who are old, I mean really old. While their bodies may look the epitome of health and fitness, their attitudes and life perspectives are humbug. For them, life is nothing but an endless series of heartache and disappointment, then they die.

But I have also had the fortune of meeting really young 90ish year olds. They see every day as vital and full of possibilities. For them, life will end too soon.

Transforming leaders and people of legacy do not allow the accumulation of calendar years to determine their attitudes about life. While there may be times of disappointment, overall they maintain an optimism about their life and future. Every day they rise to seek opportunities for meaning, learning, growing, stretching and exploring the world. Leaders bent

185

on adding value to living spend every moment as if it is their last. This is the vitality that keeps them eternally youthful.

• Is life fun or a drudgery for you? Why or why not? Do you look forward to every day and the opportunities it may afford? Why or why not?
• Are you optimistic about life? Are you excited about what is out there waiting for you? Why do you feel as you do?

Elements of a
Noble Life

Nobility is the one and only virtue.

—Juvenal
Roman poet & satirist
(AD 60-130)

I CIRCLED THE MUSICAL MEASURE with a blue pen when we finished singing. "Till all success be nobleness," read the lyric. Nobleness equals success.

What does it mean to achieve success in a noble life? If there is success in a life lived with nobility, then what are the ingredients that make for that reality? What qualities, if lived courageously, would transform your own world while impacting the lives of others?

The Apostle Paul clearly articulates the qualities of a noble life in his first-century writing to the church. By taking adequate time from your helter-skelter life to think about, plant and nurture these seven seeds of the spirit, you will create a successful, noble life.

1. Being true. Something that is true is exactly what you see when you look at the object. There is no hidden meaning, no shadow of anything behind the scenes, only exactly what you see with your eyes and heart. Objects that are true name themselves, like beauty, wisdom and wholeness. If you live with truth, then you are exactly what people see, even at first glance. When you live in truth, there is no deception, no duplicity, no changing values or ethics in you, regardless if the times are stressful or successful. Being true beckons you to think and act for the highest possible good, not only for yourself but for others as well.

2. Being honorable. In the previous century, a handshake was believed as ironclad and binding as any written contract. Being honorable is as binding as that handshake. Honor is a promise to do what is right in word and deed, even if the consequences of your decisions would be against you. When you live with honor, you bring a seriousness to your life purpose, as well as a self-respect, because your conduct is congruent with your thoughts and words. Honor lived to this degree avoids deceit of others and ourselves. Living at this commitment level also inspires awe in others and, like a beacon, attracts them to measure their own lives against this principle.

3. Being Just. When you are just, you are able to be judged right by the standards of universal principles. In pursuing a just life, you work diligently at living in perfect agreement between your very nature and your actions. Living your life justly not only sets a standard for yourself but also for others to consider for their own journey.

4. Being pure. Pursuing purity transforms us. In the ancient Greek world, purity meant being dedicated to the gods, to have a life that is not contaminated or defiled by immorality. Today's license to moral freedom is corrupting. The steady dripping of water against a rock will ultimately erode its surface. Likewise, a steady stream of immoral thoughts and actions will lead one's life to ruin. In a culture saturated with the siren's songs of immorality, being pure and chaste may be the noblest choice of all.

5. Being lovely. What would the world be like if we really loved? Oh, we "love" baseball, French fries and cars, but what if we really loved each other as intensely as we "love" these inanimate objects? Being lovely in mind, spirit and action means living an attitude that calls out the best in another human being. Lovely living is about inviting people to leave behind bitterness, cynicism and strife for a lifestyle of mercy, compassion and self-giving. By being lovely, you personally become transformed from self-indulgence to other-centeredness in your choices and responses to life circumstances.

6. Being gracious. A gracious life is known through one's words. When you are gracious, you speak about situations and those people involved in a balanced and fair manner. Gossip and unfair portrayals of other people have no place in a noble life. The true test for identifying a gracious person is they always speak about people and circumstances as if God were standing within ear-shot of each uttered syllable.

7. Being excellent. Striving for excellence is the current catch-phrase for the self-improvement movement. Yet living with excellence is more than a slogan. Being excellent means never resting from any assignment unless you know you have truthfully given your best efforts. Living excellence does not permit you to approach a task with a mind-set of what is adequate, because excellence challenges you to work to your fullest potential in all you desire to achieve. Excellence is not a once-in-a-while application of your abilities, but an all-of-the-time choice to exercise that spirit in your relationships, learning, careers and thoughts.

It seems there are two traveling companions on the journey to creating a noble life. The companion of Mistakes allows you to falter again and again while teaching you ways to make nobleness real in your life. But the second companion, Persistence, is always there to encourage and remind you that a noble character is not manifested overnight. Counting your character as noble takes root over a lifetime of attentiveness to universal principles.

If you desire to leave lasting legacies of nobleness, then you must willingly pay the price to nurture these seven elements in your soul. Living nobly ultimately exalts your character to the highest form of excellence you can encounter while alive. In the grand scheme of humanity, living this degree of conduct toward yourself and others can be recognized as no small success.

• When people say your name, does that utterance alone define you as noble, like saying the word beauty?
• Is your word ironclad, like a written contract?
• Are you pure in mind and deed?
• Do you speak as if God where listening to what you say?

Personal Excellence: An Ethical Obligation

First say to yourself what you should be;
and then do what you have to do.

—Epictetus
Greek stoic philosopher
from *Discourses*
(AD 60-117)

IN OUR CULTURE, excellence equals perfection. It is unfortunate that we have made this connection. By making this link, we paralyze ourselves, forgetting that excellence is not about perfection, but about progression to the highest human ideals.

Obtaining excellence is about a progression from an original state to something better. It is an unfolding from the present situation to what is the greatest potential or possible good.

The journey to excellence in life begins with vision. Vision is a road map, a picture of what the future should be. This road map is a mental picture that directs your actions, resources and energies toward your greatest future. This snapshot of the

191

future gives you energy to work hard at accomplishing your dreams. The Hebrew concept of excellence says that there is an "elation of the mind" when we see an excellent future. A well defined and compelling personal vision extracts personal commitment and jubilation for achieving the best.

Attaining personal excellence also means possessing the highest degree of virtue and goodness. Personal excellence focuses on qualities such as grace, purity, honesty, truth and nobility. The interesting point about possessing these characteristics is they are not only lived internally, but are conspicuous to others. Excellence means surpassing what is adequate or average. By doing so, others will also acknowledge these qualities evident in you.

Working toward excellence involves expending energy. Again, I love the Hebrew concept of excellence on this point. Excellence, in their words, contains the idea of "raging upward." When you focus on excellence, you should proceed with intense fury toward your vision. Being excellent does not mean an occasional outburst, but a constant stream of energy focused with laser intensity on the goal.

Pursuing excellence ultimately requires constant movement. Complete rest from striving, as Pascal observed, is death. The journey toward excellence is like the ascent of a mountain. While there may be set backs, barriers or delays, the climbers remain focused on the summit. Achieving excellence demands your continuing focus on the ultimate goal of reaching the highest personal good.

Tom Morris, author of *True Success*, captures the core concept of excellence when he writes:

> *I am strongly inclined to think that the most fundamental ethical obligation of excellence each of us has is an obligation to be the best that we personally can be at each and every thing that we do, across a broad range of interests and activities, given the legitimate constraints of our most basic*

natural endowments, the opportunities we've had to develop, and the other commitments it is equally good that we have.

The road to personal excellence is not about competition. Your desire for excellence should be measured against how *you* are improving. Grading yourself against others alone creates arrogance or defeat. It is more essential to gauge your progress against who you were a month, a year or a few days ago than others. That measurement is the penultimate summit.

• Do you equate excellence with perfection? If so, does that keep you from ascending the mountain of excellence?

• Are you intense about your vision? Does it extract passion in you for success?

• Are you a better person—in the sense of the highest human good—than you were a few days ago or last year? Do others recognize these qualities in you?

AUTUMN
S E A S O N

THE FALL OF THE YEAR BRINGS EXCITEMENT! It is a time of readying for school, preparing for the winter ahead and completing projects that consumed the summer. Autumn also represents the last months of the calendar year. During these months we look back on what we have accomplished during the Winter, Spring and Summer while peering forward to the change from one year to the next. In many ways, it is a season of transition, that is, it asks us to consider the culmination of all we have come to be as well as what we hope to be in the future.

The Autumn Season of leadership is a time for focusing on moving from the lessons about ourselves into the application of those lessons in our workplace or community. It is during the Autumn Season that we must apply what we are learning and understanding about ourselves. It is here that we begin to focus on liberating others to be and do their best. It is a time of transformation because, over the previous Season, we have been transformed in our capacities to lead and prepare for the future.

The final section of this book is focused on your relationships with others. In the Autumn Season, you will consider, among other attributes, your beliefs and practices related to collaboration, diversity, encouragement and hope-fulness. While the Winter, Spring and Summer Seasons have been self-focused, the Autumn Season is other-focused. It is the time in which you must apply what you have learned so that others might become what they, too, are intended to be.

In many ways, the Autumn Season lasts a lifetime. While you must always monitor your mission, learning and self-development, the real test of your leadership comes in living the Autumn Season over and over again. By living and prac-ticing the seeds of the Autumn Season, you are inviting other people to join in the journey of leadership. The astonishing fact of this invitation is that the cycle will be renewed and leaders will create leaders, who will create leaders, who will create leaders—just as the cycle of the seasons is reborn, the efforts of your leadership in the Autumn Season will produce new cycles of mission, learning, self-development and libera-tion of others in a new generation of leaders.

While it may seem that the Autumn is the end, it is just the beginning. And in that beginning, may you really know yourself and others for the first time.

RECOMMENDED BOOKS FOR THE AUTUMN SEASON:

The Leadership Challenge: How to Get Extraordinary Things Done in Organizations. James Kouzes & Barry Posner. Jossey-Bass Publishers: San Francisco. 1987

On Leadership. John W. Gardner. The Free Press: NY. 1990

The Leader of the Future. Frances Hesslebein, Marshall Goldsmith & Richard Beckhard. Jossey-Bass Publishers: San Francisco. 1996

To Be Trusted, Be Trust-worthy

If you once forfeit the confidence of your fellow citizens, you can never regain their respect and esteem.

—Abraham Lincoln
16th President of the United States
(1809-1865)

IT MUST BE A CRUEL EXPERIENCE for anyone in a position of authority to endure a "vote of confidence." Possibly having worked hard all their life, they come to the moment when the trust with their colleagues has been forfeited. What pain must be experienced the second the results are shared.

To be trusted, you must be trust-worthy. Being worthy of trust and being given the confidence of others does not happen because of position. Trust is given when there is consistency between the words and actions of the leader.

Trust is awarded to another when he or she is truthful, full of integrity and driven by principles in their lives.

The amazing part of trust is that it is not given because of grand moments in leadership. Trust is given in the little matters, such as protecting the reputation of others, being full of truth, not gossiping, being responsible and accountable in small matters, or considering the welfare of others before your own.

Once the confidence or trust we have in another is broken, we may never regain it. Our reputation is easier sustained than repaired.

- Are you a person who can be trusted? Why or why not? How do you know?
- Do you protect the reputations of others, tell the truth, show integrity in all matters and live by principle? If not, why not?
- Is it important to protect your reputation? How are you actively protecting your reputation?

Inspire Bravery
in Others

PAUL NEWMAN, IN THE MOVIE *Nobody's Fool*, is questioned by his timid grandson about being brave. Newman takes a pocket watch from his jacket and gives it to the young boy. As he hands him the timepiece, he says, "All you need to do is be brave for one or two minutes. This stop watch will help you see your courage."

Leaders are like Newman's character in the movie. They encourage people around them to be braver—just a minute longer—when the going gets tough. In times of uncertainty, leaders encourage people to remain focused on the vision as their beacon in the night.

Bravery is not embodied in the macho stereotypes of silver screen superheros. Being brave is displaying your beliefs through actions concerning a critical purpose or maintaining an unwavering stance for what is right.

We get confused in our culture about healthy personality characteristics because of the bigger-than-life images regularly shot at us. These images are not the epitome of bravery. They are only a small segment of our culture's idea of what it means to have courage.

True bravery evidenced in more subtle ways leaves lasting memories. Bravery is the image of a child standing tall against the taunting bully on the playground. It is also witnessed in a mother who proudly stands at a PTO meeting, voicing her concern for the inequity of a program that puts some children at a disadvantage. This lone voice becomes even more memorable when the child is not her own. Bravery might even wear a three piece suit, as a businessman resigns his prestigious and lucrative job because there is evidence that his employer is unethical and deceiving in most practices.

Bravery comes in all shapes and sizes of people. It can be witnessed in a person objecting to an off-color joke or a prejudiced remark, or standing alone with someone who has been treated unfairly. It is a brave person who is willing to confront another—even a hierarchical superior—when justice must receive a voice.

Opportunities for being brave are present wherever right and good are challenged by injustice, disrespect or harm. It is truly a matter of whether your convictions are strong enough to make you stand five more minutes for the right.

- Are you willing to confront people or situations that are injurious to others?
- What issues are you aware of right now that demand your bravery?
- What injustices must be brought into line with universal principles if the good of all is to be preserved?

Your Word Is
Your Bond

promise *(prom'is)* *n: an assurance*
given by one person to another that the
former will or will not do a specified act; to
give reason for expecting.

—Funk & Wagnalls Standard
Comprehensive Dictionary

WE ALL MAKE PROMISES. Our intentions are good
when we make them, but we do not always carry through on
our pledges. There may have been a time when you promised
something but for whatever reason did not carry out your
vow. Yet no matter the circumstance, what we forget is
promises contain sacred pledges of trust for keeping our
words through our actions.

Promises are a declaration of what you will do. When
you make promises, you make a public declaration that what
you say will be backed by your actions. It is a fallacy to
believe promises are secretly made. Promises gain their significance and solemn covenant when you verbalize your
intentions to another human being. When you state your
intentions, they become tangible contracts of what lies in
your heart to accomplish.

Promises also carry guarantees. When you make guarantees, you bind yourself to assuring your treasures, time and talent will be used to make your intentions real. The Greeks stated that promises were legally binding agreements. If you treat your promises with that intensity, you will make sure to deliver on what you say.

There is no middle ground and no hedging when you make promises. At the heart of these contracts is a willingness to do or not do something in the future. It is interesting that we often associate promises with doing. However, making promises may mean voluntarily limiting yourself and your actions in order that the greatest good be realized by others.

Finally, you release the best in other people when you make promises. Promises should not harm but seek the highest good for others. In the deepest sense, promises are personal gifts bestowed on others so they might succeed with your assistance.

Yet because we are human, we often unintentionally break our promises. So what must you do if you fail to keep these agreements? First, you must stop and squarely face the circumstances caused by breaking promises. Without laying blame, you must be accountable for your words and your lack of action or restraint. Second, you must seek restoration. When you seek restoration, you do everything within your power to make the situation right. This is essential for rebuilding trust. Restoration is about returning your relationships to their original state. And it is only through the third element—action—that you can rebuild trust.

When you break your promises, your words no longer carry significance. Over time, people discount or ignore your words because they have not been bolstered by action. Broken promises require the payment of continual action until others once again believe what you say is binding. But until then, your actions are essential to restoring relationships.

Promises are a sacred agreement with others about intention and action. Keeping them is critical to all leadership and all relationships.

• Do you keep your promises? Can people count on your words being backed by your actions?

• When you break a promise, are you quick to express your accountability and seek restoration, or do you pass off the situation as insignificant?

Value Action
over Rhetoric

Actions do speak louder than words.
Manuals don't count. Leadership is good
work, not simply good talk.

—Max DePree
former Chair of Herman Miller
author (from *Leadership Jazz*)

THERE IS ONLY ONE RULE: take care of the customer to the best of your judgment. That simple statement has made Nordstrom's a $4.5 billion specialty retail store.

The stories of Nordstrom's customer service are legend. The stories of overnighting clothing to clients on vacation or personally shopping for you while you sip cappuccino grace most books on customer service. What is often missing, however, is an explanation of the structure that allows that one-and-only rule to exist. Nordstrom's is not fond of manuals. Only actions count in satisfying the customers' needs.

Nordstrom's leadership focuses on doing instead of saying. They gain the respect and admiration of customers and sales associates and the disdain of competitors by placing emphasis on:

1. Providing an open door policy. Customers or front line sales staff have access to the CEO or Chair of the Board through published telephone numbers. And the CEO will answer his own telephone.

2. Decentralization through decisions made close to the customer by front line associates. Training is also not company sponsored but self-initiated and self-designed. While there may be coaching, associates must acknowledge their own deficiencies and seek the appropriate training.

3. An entrepreneurial spirit is valued at Nordstrom's. This specialty store looks for persons who want to own their own businesses. That spirit allows people to make good decisions in their areas of responsibility, because they would make the same decisions if their name was on the door.

4. Promoting from within is important. Everyone starts on the sales floor in order to learn the business.

5. Supporting relationships are critical for success. People do business with people. Employees have high expectations for working with others placed on them. If they cannot succeed in this area, they eventually drop from the company.

While Nordstrom's is a high pressure, high expectation company, they succeed because action is rewarded over adherence to the stipulations found in a thick policy manual. Effective leaders recognize and reward productivity, performance, being a team player and results. Determining whether your performance fits the manual is commonplace. Leaders who release people to work hard and be their best do so because they focus on action above all else.

- If you are prone to rhetoric over action, what will you begin doing to change this mind-set?
- Are your actions consistent with your words? If not, why? How will you make your words and actions consistent?
- Do you release people to do their jobs, coaching them when necessary, or do you cage them by the use of manuals, policies, procedures and burdensome job descriptions?

Each of Us Is
a Human Being

*Remember that the fellowship of human
beings is more important than the fellowship
of race and class and gender.*

—Marian Wright Edelman
founder of Children's Defense Fund
(from *A Measure of Success*)

TRULY VALUING AND RESPECTING THE DIVERSITY of
humankind is a corner stone of effective leadership and
building a better world.

Leadership that sees people as the fellowship of human
beings is full of courage, dignity, honor, care and respect.
This leadership never tells, laughs at, or supports racial, ethnic, religious or gender jokes or practices that demean others. Transforming leaders also confront practices and
programs or refuse conversations that unfairly limit or cen-
sure people from being what they were created to be.

If you cannot stand with courage on this issue, you cannot provide the leadership necessary for the new millennium.

- Do you tell stories or support unfair practices that demean or segregate people on the basis of race, gender, ethnic background, ability, appearance or religion? If so, why?
- Leadership for the new millennium will require courage to stand against such abuses of others. Do you have the courage? What will you begin doing this week to support people, no matter their background?

Leaders Foster the Benefits of Diversity

The body is not made up of one part but of many. If the foot should say, because I am not a hand, I do not belong to the body, it would not for that reason cease to be a part of the body. If the whole body were an eye, where would the hearing be? Or if an ear, where would the sense of smell be? As it is, there are many parts, but one body.

—The Apostle Paul
The Bible, 1 Corithians 12:14-20

THERE IS A BEAUTY IN THE DIVERSITY of the human species. The unique insights, cultural backgrounds and life experiences packaged in each person create beauty and harmony for success, whether in our organizations or the entire community.

Leaders are not only aware of the diversity that each individual brings to a given situation, but embrace it and intentionally seek the benefits that come from diverse perspectives. If we desire communities and organizations to be whole, those recognized as leaders must put forward the energy needed to include the voices of diversity.

As a society, we have been far too narrow in our definition of diversity. Often, we focus solely on culture and ethnicity when trying to include others or teach diversity to our communities. But there is great diversity between gender, personal life experiences, hierarchy, and physical abilities and appearances. One of the hardest but most critical lessons of life will be to appreciate the diversity we each bring to the various situations that occur daily. The challenge of any leader is to be cognizant of others, their feelings and the unique life perspectives they can bring to our institutions. While we often focus on skin tone, the effective leader is conscious of the subtleties that exist in each individual. Effective leaders are careful not to lump human experiences into neatly structured categories of gender, ethnic heritage or racial background.

What does all this mean for leadership and liberating people? It means that we will never move forward to a future we all desire if we are not consciously willing to foster, learn about, dialogue over and embrace the diversity that every human being brings to the world. If the janitor is not as valued for what he or she brings as the president, we will never have a liberating climate. If the black member of the community is overlooked compared to his or her white counterparts, we will never have all the energies needed for change and creativity. If the disabled are given menial tasks instead of those that require innovation, we will be doomed to a separateness and division that, like a cancer, will devour our communities.

If there is a leadership and personal character seed that may cause a person to stand alone, it is this seed of embracing diversity. If there is any ingredient that may take a lifetime to germinate, it is this seed of intentionally understanding and caring for those unlike ourselves.

In the end, the leader must be more concerned about the whole body, the whole fellowship of humanity. Leaders must make a conscious choice to build bridges that liberate and bring courage to us all. Ultimately, understanding diversity and intentionally working to accept and include others does not happen in massive demonstrations on the courthouse steps; it starts with caring about your neighbor next door.

- Have you ever taken the initiative to sit with persons different from yourself to understand their concerns, joys, values and perspectives on life?
- What makes you prejudiced against any person or group of individuals? What causes you to stereotype them?
- Are you willing to hear from all voices that make up your organization or community? From the janitor or child to the CEO?

Restore Broken Relationships through Forgiveness

Forgiveness is the key to action and freedom.

—Hannah Arendt
American author & philosopher
(1906-1975)

"I'M WILLING TO FORGIVE, but I cannot forget," is a falsehood. Believing this adage does not free either party in a wrong committed against the other. True forgiveness means you will let go of the situation, both in how you view that person now and will relate to them in the future.

Forgiveness is a restoration of relationships when a wrong is committed that breaks trust between people or communities. In forgiveness, each party has an obligation of action toward the other. It is only through mutual sharing of these actions that relationships can be restored.

A person who forgives must start with an attitude of for-giveness before another asks. If you cling to this understand-ing of forgiveness, you are able to begin restoration. But if you do not believe in forgiveness as an attitude, the barriers already exist for the improbability of wholeness to be reborn. In forgiving, you make every effort to cancel the relational debt another has against you, even if they deserve punish-ment. On our part, forgiving means we will graciously accept a person's asking for forgiveness and diligently take initiative to restore wholeness between us.

The one seeking forgiveness also has an obligation to the injured party. In seeking forgiveness, you must repent of your actions and confess them to the one you have wronged. Repenting literally means to turn 180 degrees from the direc-tion you are going. Repenting is turning your back on what you are doing and going away from it, never to do it again. Likewise, you must confess—verbally—that you have com-mitted an offense.

In confession we are freed because we acknowledge what we have done. The spoken word—in some mystical way—makes our admission concrete and real, both to ourselves and others. But as one seeking forgiveness, a verbal confes-sion is not enough. If your confession is to have lasting meaning, you must act in a way that brings restoration.

It is sometimes easier to say the words than to follow up with actions that restore relationships. After we confess—with a contrite heart—we may have to bring monetary resti-tution, seek counseling to change our behavior, give up some habit or vice, or eliminate an attitude from our thinking. While forgiving and forgiveness restore relationships, we can never minimize there may be consequences for those wrongs committed. After all, we do live in a world of cause and effect.

Forgiveness for a wrong against another or the commu-nity is never easy, but it is essential if we are to live to the highest good. It is also critical to know that forgiveness is not just a one-time event but a continuing journey to wholeness. Jesus was asked, "Should I forgive someone seven times?" His reply startles us, but is at the heart of forgiveness. In his response, Jesus said, "No, don't forgive someone seven times. Forgive them seventy-seven times." When we are able to forgive and act in ways that restore relationships, we will begin to pull each other to the spirits we were created to be.

Ultimately, living with a heart of forgiveness and not retaliation can bring freedom and abundant life—not only for ourselves but for others.

• Do you believe in "forgiving and forgetting," or do you continue to hold the memory of a wrong against you?

• Are you willing to take the initiative to restore a relationship, or do you wait for the other person to come forward?

• If you seek forgiveness, you must act differently in the future. Are you courageous enough to seek help or pay restitution as a part of finding forgiveness?

Truth and Justice

THERE ARE TWO SIMPLY HARD REMEDIES that can spell relief for many tired and overwhelmed leaders. These two practices are cross-cultural and focus on how we treat others. If leaders courageously apply the principles of truth and justice (or reciprocity) they will solve many problems that plague businesses and society.

All major religions discuss truth and justice as core values. Reflections on truth and justice may be found in passages such as Confucius' "Superior Man," the Taoist's "Three Treasures," and Judaism's "Prophets." The writers of these works ask leaders to do what is right and just. Confucius stated, "Doing right should be as natural as breathing," and "Those who know the truth are not equal to those who love it." The Hebrew prophet Micah proclaimed that justice and doing right are more desirable than sacrificing everything. Mahatma Gandhi, the great social reformer, implored people to right themselves first—to tell the truth—in order to change society through a metamorphosis of their personal lives.

Leaders who practice this principle live out truth and justice simply because it is right—not because it is politically correct or expedient for one's career. Truth is the anchor by which effective leaders relate to others and their organizations. "Truth," as Lincoln wrote, "is generally the best vindication against slander."

Truth is not a skill learned in a seminar, but a virtue which is cultivated and nurtured because it is the most important principle in holding the confidence and esteem of people. If leaders practiced this principle consistently, new trust and loyalty could be generated within a plethora of organizations. Albert Einstein sums up this principle by observing that "whoever is careless with the truth in small matters cannot be trusted with important matters."

Additionally, the Golden Rule, do unto others as you would have them do to you, is a universal code by which effective leaders live. This value statement, too, cuts across all cultures and societies. Confucius describes the importance of this principle in a story retold in his writings, *The Analects*.

> *Tzu-kung asked (his master), saying, 'Is there one word which may serve as a rule of practice for all one's life?' The master (Confucius) said, 'Is not reciprocity such a word? What you do not want done to yourself, do not do to others.'*

Treating others as we desire to be treated may solve many of our conflicts. The principle of reciprocity could find solutions to issues of compensation, equitable benefits, working conditions, profit sharing and performance evaluations. This principle could fundamentally transform the very way we operate our organizations. Leaders who lead as if people mattered understand that reciprocity is critical to the present and future success of businesses and society.

These qualities are not skills that can be taught in so many lessons or through hearing so many tapes or reading so many books. Leaders who practice truth, justice and the Golden Rule know that leading is an affair of the heart.

As you practice these principles, you will come to realize that leadership is not a matter of position, but a becoming. Your challenge is to shift your current practices in relationships to those truths that are universally essential. If you are willing to live and practice these principles, you will begin to witness new solutions to decades-old problems.

• What are tangible ways that justice might take shape within your organization?

• What might you have to do personally and organizationally for people to hear the truth?

• Would practicing the Golden Rule solve problems within your organization? If people were treated with the dignity inherent in the Golden Rule, how would they respond? What tangible practices would demonstrate the principles of the Golden Rule?

Go First,
The Right Way

*If anyone wants to be first, they must be
the very last, and the servant of all.*

—Jesus the Christ
The Bible, Mark 9:35

THERE IS SOMETHING MAGICAL about being first. Excited children often squeal "me first, me first" when the opportunity to be chosen comes their way. Adults, too, experience the emotion of being first as they wait for tickets to a movie or stand in line at a bank. McDonald's has even capitalized on the excitement of being first in their "Super Fan" advertisements. Being first fills us with happiness, pride, a sense of importance and maybe the possibility that we will get the best before others. It is fun to be first!

There is, however, another side of being first—one that we often forget. We seem to overlook the fact that being first carries the responsibility of showing someone "how it is done" or "showing them the ropes." Being first carries the responsibility of modeling the way for those in line or those who will follow in the future. Those who follow pick their queues from the one going first. They watch with interest how the one going first meets obstacles and maneuvers to overcome them.

Leadership is about going first. Leadership involves initiating activity, informing others of the way and setting an example for those who follow. Going first shows that the leader is committed to his or her beliefs—not just in words, but by their actions. As Posner and Kouzes write in their book, *Credibility*, "The ultimate test of a leader's credibility is whether they do what they say."

It is not unusual to hear the intentions of leaders couched in words like ought, should, can or might. Action, however, is the single most meaningful demonstration of what leaders believe and consider important. Doing shows that leaders are serious about their beliefs as well as those of their organizations.

There are many ways that leaders show their commitment to their beliefs and to the people who make up their organizations. Tangible commitments to beliefs are not always the lofty or noble actions we read about in the newspapers or see depicted in a prime-time "Movie of the Week."

The leader who goes first often displays care for the organization and its people in little ways—ways that are almost undetected by those they serve. Their actions speak volumes. Leaders make it a practice to demonstrate their convictions through a variety of actions, such as:

- The types of questions they ask
- Listening intently to what others say
- Protecting the causes and reputations of those not present in discussions
- Where they spend their money and that of the organization

Leaders focus their actions, beliefs and intentions on liberating the human spirit. They echo with Louis Mayer of MGM Studios, "The inventory goes home at night."

Leaders practice these subtle behaviors that speak loudly to those around them. But probably the most material of all practices is where leaders spend their time. Is it behind their desk or on the shop floor? Is it counting pennies or encouraging people? Is it sympathizing with problems, actively working to find solutions and breaking down barriers? Time and its use crystallize essential beliefs of the leader. The use of time gives credence to the critical issues of the organization.

It is through action that leaders develop their credibility. Leaders are "willing to hold themselves to the same set of standards as others. Credible leaders go first." There can be no greater summary for a leader, except possibly one other. Going first carries a tremendous responsibility. But a greater responsibility lies in the paradox that going first requires us, in the end, to go last.

In a time when it seems that everyone wants to be first—to have the best possessions, recognition or power—it appears foolhardy to be last. Yet the final test of greatness is summarized in the paradox, "whoever wants to be first, must be a servant."

Robert Greenleaf, the heralded author of *Servant Leadership*, sets before aspiring leaders what it means to serve others. For Greenleaf, leaders exist only to serve and develop the follower. As Chris Lee and Ron Zemke observe,

> *Servant leadership emphasizes service to others, a holistic approach to work, personal development and shared decision making—characteristics that place it squarely in the mainstream of conventional talk about empowerment, total quality and participative management.*

Being a servant leader means putting the organization and its people first. Servant leadership is demonstrated through the stating of goals or vision, aggressively listening to others, telling the truth and being trustworthy, assisting others in their development, caring for the well-being of all people, and in the end, sustaining the hope that both the organization and its people will reach their desired futures.

In the final analysis, truly being first and being last are really not so different after all. Those aspiring to leadership must contemplate the grand responsibility of going first and the realization they must be last—a servant to others. By seriously reflecting on the responsibility of leadership, you will return to the place from which you started, and know it for the first time.

• Are you a leader that asks questions that bring focus? Do your questions challenge people to put "first things first"?

• Are you willing to withhold your own opinion for a more appropriate time so that people will really share what is in their heart?

• Are you willing to protect others not present in discussions so that their reputation and ideas are protected and considered?

• Are you more willing to spend money for book value assets or to invest those dollars in the welfare of employees?

The Servant-Leader

The servant-leader is servant first. It all begins with the natural feeling that one wants to serve, to serve first. Then conscious choice brings one to aspire to lead. The difference manifests itself in the care taken by the servant—first to make sure that other people's highest priority needs are served.

—Robert Greenleaf
Founder of Greenleaf Center
for Servant Leadership
(1904-1990)

LARRY SPEARS, EXECUTIVE DIRECTOR of the Greenleaf Center, recently wrote about the concept of servant-leadership. He said, "Greenleaf tried to imagine a world where the people we value most highly are those who best serve others: the teacher who inspires a student, the nurse who cares for a patient, the boss who takes a few minutes to ask about an employee's sick child. Greenleaf's quest sparked the simple yet profound idea for servant-leadership. He thoughtfully created a series of questions that guided his life decisions as a servant-leader. "Do those I serve grow as people? Do they become healthier, wiser, more autonomous, and more likely to become servants themselves? And, how am I benefitting the least privileged in the group?"

Servant-leadership is about serving others. Greenleaf's words are ancient words. They are the words of all religions. They are the words that have motivated millions to change the world. The real question remains, "Is the concept changing you?"

• Do you believe in the servant-leader concept? Why or why not? Do you believe it is an achievable or worthy way to lead?

• As a leader, do the people you lead grow, become healthier, wiser, more autonomous, or likely to become leaders? If they do not, why not? If they do, how?

Listen to Understand

*Listen to people around you. A good
listening is a soothing of the heart.*

—Ptah-Hotep
Egyptian philosopher
(2400 BC)

FROM SOCIOLOGISTS TO MARRIAGE COUNSELORS,
there is an observation that listening is vital to healthy relationships. Wisdom teachers of ancient time counseled their
pupils to listen to others if they desired to find success. Being
unwilling to listen—really listen—causes us to "die while we
are still alive." Without listening, we become detached, isolated, insulated, and misunderstand what is happening
around us. Misunderstandings happen when we do not listen
well. Those misunderstandings can cause us problems or
great anxiety as a result.

My wife took the telephone call from our neighbor. Her
husband, who worked at a local hospital, had received a ham
as a gift from that employer. They called to invite us to dine
with them in the next hour.

Within minutes, our wide eyed, anxious eight-year-old
son appeared in the kitchen of our home. My wife shared we
were going to have dinner with the neighbors. With appre-
hension my son exclaimed, "Mom, we can't go! John got a
hand from the hospital and it's in the oven!" After a burst of
laughter, we assured our son that "cooked hand" was not on
the menu. Mental terror was the result of our son's misunder-

standing what he heard while playing at our neighbor's home. That mental image still gives us amusement to this day.

Communications experts tell us there are barriers to effective listening. These barriers deal with the loss of concentration, being distracted, or simply tuning out. The bottom line is that the major barrier is self-focused—we just do not want to hear what another person says, or we are so preoccupied with our own opinions that we shut out what others need to say.

Likewise, effective listening is other-focused. Listening that is other-focused concentrates on the speaker. This listening takes the time to watch the speaker's eyes, hear his or her opinions and become actively involved in the dialogue. Effective listening is simply caring enough, respecting enough and wanting enough to understand someone else.

By striving to find understanding through listening, we will soothe a person's heart. St. Francis of Assisi said, "It is better to seek to understand, than to be understood." Leaders who liberate people listen closely and intimately to their concerns, ideas, fears and hopes. Through the courageous act of listening for understanding, leaders create the trust necessary for interdependent relationships.

- Are you a good listener? Why or Why not?
- What would be the outcomes in your personal relationships if you were a better listener? What would be the outcomes in your place of work?
- What keeps you from being other-focused in a conversation? What is necessary for you to share your thoughts and opinions, but not to be hospitable to someone else?

Knowledge Sharing

The law of life should not be the competition of acquisitiveness, but cooperation, the good of each contributing to the good of all.

—Jawaharlal Nehru
First Prime Minister of India
(1889-1964)

COACHING AND TEAM BUILDING are a staple of how to release people's best for accomplishing organizational mission. Yet more than the element of "teamness," effective leaders plant the seeds of collaboration. Bringing people together to perform at their best is not solely applying the mechanics of team building, but more an art form characterized by collaboration.

The heart of collaboration is the cooperation and interconnectedness of people working together. Building effective organizations means planting seeds of cooperation, participation and interdependency.

Collaboration means working together toward a desired goal, much as two or more persons sharing their best efforts to write a book or create a piece of art. Like a great masterpiece, leaders work at building a collaborative environment, one in which legacies derive from the efforts of many nameless contributors and not necessarily a lone champion.

229

Collaboration involves creating an atmosphere where innovative ideas can be shared, sketched, molded and reshaped into outcomes that make the organizational mission a reality. The collaborative sharing of knowledge creates an environment aglow with energy. It is a place where people do not hoard what they know but openly feed their ideas to others, believing that sharing spins off a new thought previously not considered. Discussion, dialogue, conversation and spontaneous meetings are both welcomed and encouraged so that needed ideas become commonplace.

Collaborative environments also provide a haven for risk-taking. They are places where people are not harmed for their ideas, even if they seem foreign to the enterprise. Often, in a non-collaborative environment risk-taking is rewarded with punishment, ultimately killing creative innovation. Leaders with a collaborative mind-set nurture an environment where risks are taken, while any corrections made are for instruction, not penalty. In this environment, the vision is always the target. Any subsequent critique is meant to keep the organization on track, not to stifle an individual or the process. While there is a delicate balance between instruction and no accountability for anyone, leaders work to establish a structure that errs on the side of encouraging risk-taking.

Additionally, structures where critique of ideas and risk-taking are encouraged prevent the institution from drifting away from its intended purposes. A collaborative pair of authors once shared they need each other in writing their fictional books. This collaboration was essential because one author might spot an attitude or act of a character that is incongruent with who they have become to that point in the story. While the one writing about the character might not see the discrepancy, the other can readily see the emerging pattern and offer course correction to move the plot to its intended goal. Leaders who value collaboration know that a variety of perspectives are useful in keeping the organization moving toward the vision.

Collaborative environments also show appreciation for each other's strengths and weaknesses. As there are complimentary colors, so different talents and unique perspectives are valued and developed in enterprises intent on collaboration. In a world as vast and complex as ours, a unity and respect of other's strengths and weaknesses will grow the best possible solutions.

Heart-sensitive leaders can gauge when morale, productivity and energy are low. Leaders find ways to encourage and care for those dry in spirit, ideas or energies. Leaders developing collaboration encourage people to come to the aid of others in these times of personal dryness. The Greek word paraclete best describes this collaborative behavior. A paraclete is literally "the one who stands along side." A paraclete is one who exhorts or gives encouragement to another. It is easy for individual team members to become consumed by daily activities and stresses. Leaders must become paracletes, ones who encourage others in the dry days of the soul. In an important spiritual way, without encouragement, the whole organization is diminished when the weaker is overwhelmed by current complexities. Leaders bent on collaboration sense this dip in energy and rally others to support that person when it is needed most.

The end result of building a collaborative environment is interdependency. This interdependency is like the working of medications. While one drug may fight an infection, it may not be enough to relieve a patient's aches and pains or save their life. An interdependency of people, like medications cooperating together, can bring recovery, health and well-being. This interdependency values what each person brings to the enterprise, particularly as it breeds the best future for everyone.

- Do you really have collaboration in your workplace or merely a conglomeration of team techniques?
- Are you a paraclete—an encourager—fostering the value of every person? Are you willing to stand beside those who are in the dry deserts of their souls?
- Do you desire to be a leader who fosters collaboration and interdependency, or do you favor rugged individualism to get the job done? Why?
- Are you willing to put in the necessary time and effort—over the long term—to create institutions that build an interdependency among people? Why or why not? What will you do immediately to begin creating opportunities for collaboration?

Be a Conversational Leader

Come now, let us reason together.

—Isaiah, the Prophet
The Bible, Isaiah 1:18

SHE WAS UNBELIEVABLY MAD. She screamed and cried in a rage as we drove home in the car. Calming myself, I began to engage my three-year old granddaughter in a dialogue about what was wrong. In a matter of three short blocks, she was calm, relaxed and returned to her jovial nature. Through no more than five minutes of conversation, a toddler shared her frustrations, anger and what was hurting her.

Dialogos, that is, to speak through to a meaning, is an essential part of leadership. A freeing of the soul happens when we talk with others in soothing conversation. Like the rhythmic rocking of a mother and child, a gentle conversation can bring healing and understanding to people as they work and share together.

Leaders work to find and establish ways for people to talk together. Often, leaders focus on the big retreat, the expensive consulting sessions or the high drama of strategic thinking in order to gain needed insight about the happenings of the organization. But talking together can sow

233

and reap ideas or personal commitment untapped by other possibly sterile techniques.

Conversations can begin in seemingly unimportant locations, such as cafeterias, hallways, parking lots or at the water cooler. Leaders start conversations wherever people are gathered, all in an attempt to enlist their ideas and their spirit for the work at hand. In its deepest sense, conversational leaders intentionally create ways of listening and sharing with members of the organization. It is through this sharing together that leaders begin to truly experience the workplace, not through their own preconceived notions, but through the eyes and ideas of its people.

In addition to initiating conversation, the effective leader pays attention to the contents of the dialogue. These leaders seek out stimulating questions, answers and perspectives to help them understand the organization. Leaders focus their questions on contents that further the organization, such as what is legacy, how are you personally committed to excellence, and what role will each person play in the enterprise's success? It is in this talking together that a vivid picture of the future emerges for both leader and follower.

Conversational leaders know about their organizations beyond factual data, statistics and growth charts. Effective leaders know their enterprises experientially by dialoguing with its members. Conversation, then, becomes a constant source of insight through the exchange of ideas, the checking of assumptions and the understanding of others' viewpoints.

Conversational leaders take the time to know not only about the larger organization, but persons' names, the status of their families, lives and careers. It is through these personal conversations that workers come to believe that the leader is truly one of them.

It is a sad commentary on leadership, but I have heard it repeated by many people. With dismay and even a bit of detachment, I have talked with people who realize their own leaders do not know their names. The indifference shown on their face comes from the repeated encounters with leaders who look at them, yet only acknowledge them through some faint attempt at recognition. Leaders in touch with organizational life know not only the latest financial information but who is hurting, leaving or celebrating.

Conversation takes an investment of time, a willingness to listen and a deep desire to know the organization and its people. In the end, conversation and listening are natural ways to soothe the soul.

- When taking a walk through your enterprise, try engaging people in dialogue with questions like: Why was our organization founded? What were the important issues or concepts to our founders? Why did they create the products, services or agendas of this organization?

- Consider asking people, What personal legacy would you like to leave as a part of having been associated with this organization? What legacy should this organization be leaving to our community?

- Beyond the organizational questions, do you ever just stop, say hello and chat? Do you ask: How are your children? How is life? Do you really want to know the answers the person gives?

Your Leadership Covenant

*Covenant relationships induce freedom.
A covenantal relationship rests on shared
commitment to ideas, to issues, to values, to
goals and to management process. They are
an expression of the sacred nature of
relationships.*

—Max DePree
former Chair of Herman Miller
author (from *Leadership is an Art*)

LEADERS AND FOLLOWERS hold between themselves
a solemn and sacred agreement. In that agreement, leaders
and followers bind themselves to their promises and intentions so that their efforts might produce a reality beneficial
to all members.

This covenant relationship exists between a number of
people. The covenant surely exists between the leader and
the organization, but it also exists between leader and peer,
and between the leader and the community he or she serves.
No matter if leaders understand or acknowledge this sacred
agreement, they are governed by it nonetheless.

Covenants are a mutually understood set of intentions and obligations for working and living together. These intentions are deeply held expectations and agreements related to words and actions of both leader and follower. Yet sadly, once covenants are broken, distrust, suspicion, self-preservation, low morale and fear may grow in this relational void.

Every covenant is filled with obligations and intentions that all parties agree they will be measured against. Of the many nuances contained in the word covenant, there are six seeds at the core of this solemn agreement.

1. Trust. The very fiber of all relationships is trust. The seed of trust can never be understated. Covenants require both parties to trust the other to be who they say the are. Additionally, both partners work diligently not to neglect or shrink from their assigned or implied responsibilities. It is this unspoken, unwritten document of trust that keeps an organization together as a single unit.

2. Respect. Leaders covenant with followers to respect the areas in which they work and have responsibility. Yet respect is not simply about giving another adequate space to work without interruption. Respect is demonstrating an esteem for the work that individual performs. To respect someone is to see them as capable of excellence, not only in their assigned functions, but as a human being. Respecting people means realizing and acknowledging that no task is menial or at the bottom of worth in the grand scheme. Truly giving respect catapults leaders to view people as having worth.

From the vantage point of respect, leaders do all they can to honor and support others. When leaders respect people, they are hospitable to more than those like themselves. Additionally, hospitable leaders view the unusual person or the ideas they generate as necessary ingredients for a healthy and thriving organization. If a leader really acts with respect, he or she will provide opportunities for everyone, while establishing a climate where inclusion and participation are the cornerstone of all efforts.

3. Support. We often consider support merely giving a listening ear or a helping hand. But building a supportive climate is one in which leaders become advocates. Broader than just lending a hand, this advocacy means doing what is possible to keep a person from failing or declining in their self-worth or in their worth to the organization.

This covenantal support is sustained and continual, not given only once in a person's tenure. Support that transforms organizations and human beings is risky business. The support needed in every covenant is hard to achieve unless there is a commitment to and belief in the inherent worth of everyone. If leaders believe the common good is only achieved through a supportive atmosphere, they will take the necessary steps to demonstrate the need for it.

4. Protection. Protecting others may seem foreign to us. Yet liberating leaders know that when others come under attack, it diminishes them as people, increasing the likelihood they will become unproductive. Leaders care about protecting those within the institution, whether physically or psychologically.

Physical protection is about developing and sustaining systems and structures that ensure corporal well-being. Workplace safety, physical surroundings and managing work hazards are important issues. Additionally, while establishing systems and structures for physical safety, leaders maintain a climate that fosters concern for overall wellness. Whether you have the authority to appropriate money for risk management or not, leaders care that the health of others is secure.

Beyond maintaining physically safe environments, leaders work just as diligently to protect people from psychological attack. Gossip is the normal channel for sharing hearsay and the scoop about people. Leaders protect others by not fostering or participating in these avenues of communication. Additionally, leaders do not tolerate abuses that often occur in the hierarchical structure. If necessary, leaders are willing to stand in the gap between a person and the structure to insure protection of the individual. Leaders also join in the necessary battles to break down barriers or conditions that would injure or harm a person.

All-Pro NFL great Rosey Grier once shared, "When someone speaks against race or other people and yet we stand silent, we are telling those around us we agree with them. We cannot do it. We must speak up and be counted." Leaders are willing to both protect and be counted in the battles that would diminish the dignity of another human being.

5. Accountability. Accountability is rooted in the field of mathematics and finance. To be accountable is to literally give a reason or reckoning of why an account stands as noted. The essence of accounting is to show that all debits and credits match and are in balance.

Being accountable is a ledger of promises made and promises kept. Leaders know that the balance must be equal if people are to find faith and trust in them. Being accountable means one can count on what is said and done by the leader. Leaders make a solid connection between what ought or should be done and what is.

Leaders know they are not only responsible to the hierarchical structure but to the people that compose the organization. Because of this belief, leaders are open to assessment and evaluation by others. Leaders are vulnerable to the group, taking responsibility for mistakes and errors that might fall within their control, never shifting blame or looking for a scapegoat when circumstances go sour.

Being accountable also means being willing to confront when conflicts and disagreements arise. Leaders do not withdraw from conflict but know that it is a necessary part of a healthy environment. Just as an audit is needed to balance and correct accounts, so conflict may bring the action, obligations and expectations of others into line with the mission.

Accountability is a hard seed to plant. Accountability requires that leaders take personal risk by placing themselves on the line of public scrutiny for their deeds and their words. It also mandates that leaders keep their own egos in check.

Pride and ego that place the leader above accountability to others are dangerous journal entries to the ledger.

6. Fidelity. The all encompassing element of covenant relationships is fidelity. It is probably the most spiritual and passionate of all covenant characteristics. In a covenantal relationship, fidelity contains the sacred vows that leaders and followers make to each other. As a strong and healthy marriage, leaders and followers see each other as partners who deserve loyalty, truthfulness, consistency and allegiance. The allegiance—one for the other—is ironclad, bound by a strict adherence to truth. The covenant is ultimately sealed by the leader's reliable actions in faithfully carrying out his or her responsibilities, whether publicly or privately. In all things, the relationship between leaders and those that follow comes first.

The fidelity of covenant also requires leaders to place the welfare of others before their own personal agendas or narrow perspectives on what is best. In fidelity, the leaders constantly reflect on the tension between their own personal motives and how their decisions might enhance the needs of the followers first.

This spiritual seed of covenant ultimately ends in an unfailing commitment of the leader to those they serve. Above all things, leaders are concerned about building enterprises that promote the best for all members. The fidelity of leader to follower can produce an atmosphere of high performance, where people respond because they are treated as adults, not being watched and nursed through every responsibility and assignment. In fidelity, leaders and followers transcend what is contractually obligated to a relationship that blooms because of the deep loyalty that can exist one for the other.

Central to the concept of covenant is the mutual obligation of each partner for the other. Rooted in the garden of truth, each party agrees to uphold their duties so that harmony, peace and prosperity might be the result of their combined actions. In a time when suspicion, doubt, broken promises and fear are the norm, leaders must prepare organizations to accept the excellence found in covenantal relationships. It is by being wholly present—body, soul and mind free of distractions—that leaders will demonstrate their covenant with others, as well as their personal interest in everyone's present and future.

- Are you respectful of every human being, no matter their station in life?
- Are you a person who supports people and protects them both physically and psychologically? Would you be willing to go the distance to protect people and secure their welfare?
- Would you be willing to make yourself accountable to the entire organization and its constituents? Are you willing to have your promises and actions audited to determine if they are in balance?
- As a leader, do you acknowledge the covenant that exists between the follower and leader? Are your relationships filled with trust, respect, support, protection and mutual accountability?
- What does it mean to be faithful—to live in fidelity—with those in your organization? What changes would it make in your life or the lives of those around you?

Be a Source
of Hope

Hope is the thing with feathers that
perches in the soul and sings the tune
without the words and never stops at all.

—Emily Dickinson
American poet
(1830-1886)

LEADERS WHO STAND IN THE GAP between people's current reality and the future bring almost a metaphysical quality
of optimism about what could be. If people are to find brighter
paths to the future, leadership must provide a sense of hope that
there is a finer life awaiting them. It is the torch of hope held
high by the leader that almost makes them charismatic.

All in all, as Napoleon observed, leaders are merchants
of hope. As merchants, leaders not only peddle visions of a
superior future but become architects of the structures that
make those dreams real.

Hope is belief in things not seen. It is by hope that our
minds visualize our desired future while our hearts ooze out
the passionate work that make it concrete. And it is the
leader who keeps them both alive.

Victor Frankl's book, *Man's Search for Meaning,* is a profound writing on the ingredient of hope. The book is his personal story of Nazi concentration camps and the suffering people endured at the hands of their captors. Frankl writes of prisoners who lost faith and hope in the future and would find a way to "hit the wire." That phrase was the euphemism for those that committed suicide by grabbing the electrical fencing running around the camps. Those who lost their belief in the future were doomed, wrote Frankl. Death came swiftly when prisoners lost their hope for living and surviving to tell the world of their suffering.

Throughout his years at Dachau and Auschwitz, Frankl came to understand Friedrich Nietzsche's words that "he who has a why to live can bear with almost any how." Frankl affirmed that when we have hope and are encouraged by others to live in that hope, we can bear much.

We innately know there is a better life for ourselves, our families, the institutions and communities we serve. As John Gardner writes, "Humans have always lived partly on present satisfaction, partly on hope. And it's the task of the leader to keep hope alive. It is the ultimate fuel." Hopeful leadership ignites those beliefs that can set the world ablaze.

• Are you an optimistic and hopeful person? If yes, what makes you so? If not, why?

• Hopeful leaders see barriers as opportunities. Do you see the opportunities around you and others? Do you ask what are the opportunities? Are you more likely to leave people in wishful thinking or challenge them to the solutions?

The Power of Invitation

I have a dream today . . . . When we let freedom ring, when we let it ring from every village and every hamlet, from every state and every city, we will be able to speed up that day when all of God's children, black men and white men, Jews and Gentiles, Protestants and Catholics, will be able to join hands and sing in the words of the old Negro spiritual, "Free at last! Free at last! Thank God Almighty, we are free at last!

—Martin Luther King Jr.
Civil Rights Leader and minister
(1929-1968)

POSITIONAL LEADERSHIP OFTEN RESORTS to the use of power, control, command, force or fear in motivating people to accomplish a kaleidoscope of tasks that they deem worthy. Interestingly enough, many logical and reasonable people do what they are told because of a perceived or real upper hand of position, personal influence or intimidation possessed by the leader. Additionally, people may respond to a leader's command out of fear or a desire not to be harmed in some way, be it physically, emotionally, economically, politically or socially. While it may be impolite to talk openly about wielding power and control, it is no secret many leaders use it for one simple reason—it works.

Yet the use of power presents a haunting question that demands a legitimate answer. We must ask, "What happens in the long run to people who are commanded, controlled, or pressured to complete tasks through the exercise of raw power?" It seems likely that leaders who daily use power alone to generate compliance ultimately create a climate that elicits low self-esteem, anxiety, a "dying eight hours every day" or just a woeful resignation that this is life.

It is naïve to believe that power, command or control should never be used, especially in times of crisis or emergency. But in today's society, people are seeking stimulating and inspiring avenues for adding meaning and purpose to their lives. Many people hunger to have their work, energies and actions count for something more than an hourly wage. It is also a time in our culture when a whole generation is unimpressed with the transparent display of power to accomplish "what is good for us all." Leaders can no longer command people to do their work, without question, while loving their assignment. Today's response from people of all ages and backgrounds is stress overload, harm to others, apathy, or inaction. Positional leaders, because of their power base, may be able to buy a person's physical motion in a span of an eight-hour day, but people freely give their hearts and minds only by choice.

Maybe it is time for leaders to put away the prevailing power paradigm and in turn invite people to join in the causes that are meaningful for families, organizations, and communities.

Offering an invitation may sound cowardly, weak or uncontrollable. Yet leaders who believe that command, control and power are the only methods of enlisting people's actions do not understand the power of invitation. It only takes a few moments in observing the lives of followers to major world religions or devotees to cult activities to comprehend the lessons of invitation. People change completely, give every penny of their possessions and willingly die for the causes they believe in, whether it looks rational or logical to the casual observer. Invitation is a powerful summons.

Invitations deliver a message calling people to come somewhere or do something for an intended reason. With alluring and gracious asking, an invitation is meant to beckon a person out of their normal routine or current mind-set to be a part of something exciting, different or passionate. An invitation may be to adventure, an undertaking that involves risk, an opportunity to accomplish a grand event or the call to be a part of something extraordinary. The power of invitation can be life changing.

Leaders who are interested and committed to unleashing the power of the human spirit can look to the mission statement as an invitation. If leaders need the freewill offering of people's time, talent and treasures, then they should form an invitation that is clear, meaningful and passionate.

Mission statements are standard operating practice for people, organizations and communities. Yet many missions are stale, unappealing, uninspiring and uninviting. To capture the human spirit, leaders must create, clarify and hone a mission that is not fixed on the short-term, but on the legacy-building longed for by the soul. In order to author a compelling mission, leaders need to visualize a clear picture of the desired future grounded in a concept of universal principles.

Once the picture is framed, a leader diligently works to find the words that portray a call to participation and action. Additionally, these words must be inspiring not only to the leader but to those invited to aid in accomplishing the inherent goals of the mission.

Many invitations through mission are disregarded or ignored because the mission is about increasing marketshare or profit, creating advantages for select individuals or realizing some pet leadership interest. If leaders hope to capture people's minds, hearts and imaginations, they must engrave an invitation that will enlist a person's participation through free will. In reality, an inspiring invitation is less about temporal concerns and more about what we can accomplish for the common good as we strive to become what we are meant to be as human beings.

Abraham Lincoln could have laid out the government's strategic plan for rebuilding a country destroyed by Civil War, all the while telling the North and South to relinquish their angers. But instead, Lincoln humbly summoned all citizens of this country to have no malice toward another, express charity to all and to "bind up the nation's wounds; to care for him who shall have borne the battle; and for his widow and orphans—to do all which may achieve and cherish a just and lasting peace, among ourselves and all nations."

Martin Luther King Jr. could have listed and demanded that injustices, low pay and segregation be righted in a legal document with all the associated stipulations. But instead, King boldly challenged us to create a nation that would "rise up and live out the true meaning of its creed: We hold these truths to be self-evident that all men are created equal." Not only did King invite people to uphold our nation's creeds, but passionately summoned this country to live by justice, character, community, brotherhood and true freedom.

Jesus could have pronounced that all humans are corrupt, needing to get their act together. But instead, in serenity Jesus beckoned humankind to come and eat at a banquet table heaped with the trimmings of abundant life—a magnificent table where every tear would be wiped away, every hurt healed and every parching thirst quenched.

Laboring diligently to plant the ideals of what our lives can be will engage the human spirit and tap the fountains of human potential. It must be less about the scarcity of and competition for profits and more about the economic well-being of all people. It must be less about gaining individual worth and power and more about human prosperity. It must be less about having a nice, cozy place to live and more about a community that provides opportunities and liberation for all of its citizens.

Once the picture is clearly viewed, its energy will explode when passionately preached—not shared, not talked about, not politely discussed in conversation but preached. Preaching the mission with clarity and a strong, unwavering voice will deliver people to its ideals. A principle-centered mission is, after all, an invitation that summons us to create a better life, legacy, society and planet, not just for a few but for all who hear its message.

The consuming power of invitation is that the receiver has to make a freewill choice. People may choose to respond favorably to the summons, or they may ignore the calling. If they ignore it, that is their right, because it is their choice. If organizations and communities are to be transformed or to transcend the status quo, they must summon the energies of those from all ages, economic groups, races and abilities. If transformational leaders really hope to offer opportunities and a quality of life to more than a few, they will work endlessly to preach the mission.

And if the invitation is discarded by persons with abilities or means, leaders are obligated to send the request again. Only this time the summons will be sent, not to those who ignored the call with some flimsy excuse, but to those who have the ears to hear, a willing heart to say "yes" and a passionate commitment for realizing the transformation.

The invitation to build healthy, liberating and successful families, neighborhoods, organizations, communities and nations will be accomplished, not because leaders command it to be so. Our deepest hopes for the future will become real only because the human spirit was invited to participate in dreams that are life altering.

- Does your mission provide hope and an invitation for people to give their lives to something worthwhile?
- Are you willing to preach the message of the mission to anyone willing to listen?
- Do you prefer the use of power and command to the power of an invitation? Why?

Small and Simple Kindnesses

Life is made up, not of great sacrifices or duties, but of little things in which smiles and kindness and small obligations given habitually, are what win and preserve the heart and secure comfort.

—Joseph Joubert
French philosopher & writer
(1754-1824)

OUR CULTURE THRIVES ON THE BIG SCORE. Whether it is in seeking our fortune or in accomplishing some magnificent deed, we look for grand victories to give our lives meaning. We do the same with encouragement. We falsely believe that if the present isn't big enough or noticeable enough, it is not worth giving.

I love to collect stories of encouragement. They are helpful to me when I am trying to illustrate for a seminar audience the power of encouragement. One story I repeatedly tell is about a manager who had responsibility for a large clerical pool. He really wanted to find ways to reward their productivity, but did not always have the financial means. Finally, he was notified that he would receive money to replace all the desk chairs for the pool. Having the mind-set of empowerment, he saw the opportunity to create encouragement with the purchase of these new chairs.

One day after the chairs arrived, he stepped from his office and said, "Mary (not her name), please come to my office." With a hush that fell like dew over the office, Mary quietly made her way through the maze of desks.

Inside his office, the manager told Mary to take a seat. Waiting to be criticized, Mary was overcome when her manager began to praise her for the hard work and initiative she was demonstrating. And with that, he brought out a new office chair from behind his desk, had Mary sit in it and wheeled her through the office back to her desk! While I don't know the outcome of the productivity in the days that followed, I believe it would be a safe bet that it increased one hundred percent.

You see, even as adults we really are just like the child who paints a picture for a family member who, on seeing it, praises us, celebrates with us and hangs it on the refrigerator. As adults, we really do want people to praise us when we do good work. That desire never goes away. The child inside every person craves encouragement and recognition. We all want our bosses to take our hard work and hang it on the filing cabinet for every one to see! But instead, it may often be received with a grunt and filed away for some other more appropriate adult review.

Stickers are a great reward. I place stickers on papers and tests of my students when they do good work. I have been using stickers in my college courses for over six years. It is fun to listen to the responses of these college students when I return their papers during class. "I got a sticker! Did you get one?" passes with hushed tones around the room when the papers are received. Student scores always seem to increase over the course of the semester as they work to get stickers. While most packs of stickers or stars cost me no more than two dollars, they are liberating rewards of recognition. You see, these college students are no different than when they went to first grade and received a star on a paper. Again, the issue is, as we all mature, we forget that childlike enthusiasm and desire for recognition never goes away.

Leaders who liberate people know it is the daily dispensing of small kindnesses that encourage, comfort and lift one's burdens. Monumental sacrifices may sustain people's energy for a day, a week or even a year. But the small victories of life, heaped upon each other, sustain our momentum for a lifetime.

• Are you always seeking ways to accomplish a magnificent deed for yourself or others? Why? What will you achieve, for the long term, from that event or action?

• What actions, if performed daily, will liberate people to be and do their best? If you need assistance in thinking of small ways to celebrate with people, purchase Bob Nelson's book, *1,001 Ways to Praise Employees*.

Recognize Other's Efforts

It is the greatest of all mistakes to do nothing because you can only do a little. Do what you can.

—Sydney Smith
English clergyman & essayist
(1771-1845)

HAND-WRITTEN NOTES are a little gesture in the reward and recognition industry. It may be why we forget these little acts of encouragement during the daily hustle. Yet a simple "Thank you" and small acts of praise are enough to elevate someone's spirit.

In 1994, I created my own Society to thank people for their contributions and work with students, faculty and staff on our university campus. I founded my own recognition program with the purchase of a five dollar package of bordered laser paper and a few minutes of time. I have inducted 69 members into my Society since its beginning. Each semester I select the inductees and send them a certificate suitable for framing.

I also send a note along with the certificate that explains the award and expresses my thanks. In this short note, I share congratulations.

> *Dear Inductee to the Society of the Soaring Raven,*
>
> *Congratulations! You have been inducted into the Society of the Soaring Raven. The enclosed certificate carries no money, no promotion, no public awards banquet, and no halo. But it does carry my belief that Anderson University has some of the finest people within its halls. While I too carry no particular authority, I do carry thanks for what you have given to this institution. In watching you over the past semester, I have come to understand the human value you personally bring to this school through your example of service.*
>
> *Thanks for what you do for Anderson University! I count it a privilege to be your peer and colleague in this endeavor to transform the lives of students. You now join 69 other members of this Society since its creation in 1994.*

The responses to this recognition have been wonderful. I often see these laser printed certificates hanging on walls as I walk around our campus. I also receive appreciation notes, like these:

> *You made my day! I'm proud to be a "Soaring Raven." Thanks for the kudos!*
>
> *I really appreciate the certificate of the Society of the Soaring Ravens. What a nice*

gesture. It's just nice to be appreciated, and it made my day.

I just wanted to thank you for inducting me into the Society of the Soaring Raven. I'm truly honored that you thought of me.

Thank you for awarding me with the Society of the Soaring Raven certificate. It made my day, and it hangs on my office wall.

You possess the power to make a little thing a great thing. Being creative in thanking people for what they do can be liberating. Do what you can to recognize others. The greater crime is to do nothing at all.

- Do you believe that little gestures of appreciation can liberate the human spirit?
- Are you sincere in your encouragement? Does it come out of your character, or is it just a showy technique you use?

Create a Community

Man is a special being, and if left to himself, in an isolated condition, would be one of the weakest creatures; but associated with his kind, he works wonders.

—Daniel Webster
American orator & statesman
(1782-1852)

"WE NO LONGER TALK just about the neighbor next door," observed The First Lady of Indiana, Judy O'Bannon, "but about those that live in our virtual communities." The virtual community, she explained, is global in nature, people connected not by the backyard fence but by the marvel of computers.

In the virtual world, we know people as we can only know them through cyberspace. Their computer address, telephone number, age and credit line stand as the foundation of our interactions and relationships. It is in cyberspace that we can also be who we want because we are who we create on the video monitor. The dismal part of these relationships beyond the lack of contact is we "talk" only until our telephone bill is excessive or we become bored. At either point, we terminate our connection to that someone in the virtual community by turning off the computer and walking away.

Not only are our cyber communities fractured and impersonal, the communities within our own organizations are becoming virtual as well. Most institutions today conduct a great deal of business via computers and voice systems. These are marvelous tools of efficiency and aid in freeing time for the average worker. But these technological marvels also separate us from the person in the next office or down the hall. Cyberspace also creates an impersonal culture within the very institutions we lead.

Leaders must work tirelessly to create and sustain community. Communities are places where people share values, instruction about mores, involvement, growth and life together. In a community, people also care about each other's well-being.

Leaders are an essential element for the building and sustaining of community. Leaders create and build structures that make involvement with others more than connections through a twisted pair of telephone lines. Healthy organizational structures and environments have key elements for keeping the sense of community alive and thriving. These structures demonstrate:

- A belief in the power of diversity through all people
- Open communication of ideas, projects and financial health
- Conflict resolution as a necessary part of living together
- The value of collaboration, consensus and partnerships for innovation and problem solving
- A deep level of trustworthiness and integrity
- Personal accountability and responsibility
- Celebration for the common life we share together
- Care for the personal welfare and wholeness of others

Healthy communities do not leave these activities and structures to chance. Transformational leaders model and build avenues for nurturing interaction between neighbors. Some examples might be:

- Having quarterly family picnics or get togethers
- Holding staff meetings just to "do lunch" without a business agenda
- Using internal e-mail for recognition of people, requests for help or sharing ideas
- Holding regular "State of the Organization" addresses where people learn firsthand about the health of the company
- Inviting everyone to participate in visioning and goal-setting activities
- Holding ethnic heritage days where all groups can share their heritage and culture

One aspect leaders must encourage and role model is celebration. Celebration does not always require large demonstrations of fanfare, but there should be times of extravagance for expressing community and the interconnectedness of people.

The word celebration concerns rejoicing. To rejoice literally means to be thoroughly joyous. When we celebrate, our entire being should resonate with joy, gladness and respect for the dignity of others. Celebrations are times when people together experience victory, success, achievement and excellence. Organizations approaching community recognize celebration—both institutionally and personally—as central to their well-being.

Ultimately, communities are places where we care for each other. I have been privileged to spend most of my career at Anderson University. It is a place of faith, hope and legacy. While it is not a utopian community, it is an environment where care and concern for others is regularly witnessed.

We hold a monthly managers meeting at my institution. During opening comments at one such gathering, our Director of Conferencing spoke with confidence and optimism about a discovery and life-changing event taking place for her.

Cheryl had discovered in the prior week she had no vision in her left eye. A woman of hope and faith, she contacted a physician to examine her eye. After several consultations and tests, doctors told Cheryl she had a tumor inside her eye that would require removing the eyeball.

The room sat silently in shock. After a few questions, the managers in the room left their seats and surrounded Cheryl for a prayer of healing and wholeness. At the end of the business meeting, a waiting line formed as hugs, tears and well wishes were individually expressed to her.

I talked with Cheryl shortly after her surgery. She shared with me that over 100 Get Well cards had arrived at her home in addition to flowers and wonderfully prepared meals. Some of the cards she received came from persons she had worked with only occasionally. Nevertheless the writers expressed their hopes for restoration and wholeness.

Cheryl expressed deep gratitude for living and being a part of a community that cares for each other. While not always living to perfection, it is a place that models the words of Jesus, "For I was hungry and you gave me something to eat, I was thirsty and you gave me something to drink, I was a stranger and you invited me in, I needed clothes and you clothed me, I was sick and you looked after me, I was in prison and you came to visit me."

Creating and sustaining community is an act of courage and belief in the interconnectedness of us all. The virtual community may be efficient, but it will never replace the wonder of human fellowship.

• Looking at your organization, how does it rate as a community when comparing it with the ingredients of a community listed earlier?

• Is the place in which you work caring and considerate of others? If not, how might you become a role model for others through the acts of celebration and care for others?

What Is Transformational Leadership?

What matters is the love you put into what you do.

—Mother Theresa
nun & leader of the Sisters of Charity,
Calcutta, India
(1910-1997)

IT IS AWKWARD TO SPEAK OF LOVE in the workplace or in our communities. We often consider love sentimental and romantic. This romantic notion or the threat of a lawsuit keeps us from displaying the very essence of this word.

We also use the word love flippantly, so it tends to lose its impact. We love baseball, food or a favorite vacation spot. We would also love to get our hands on someone that offends us. This casual or sentimental use of the word love diminishes the message and character it must produce in us.

Even the dictionary definition of love leaves us wanting. For definition purposes, love is considered a strong and complex feeling causing us to appreciate or crave the presence of another. Love is also equated with affection, attraction and passion.

But love is more than all these attempts at definition. Great love is in the best interest of others. It is a mind-set and freewill choice to see the infinite preciousness of another human being. True love is unconditional, demanding no prerequisites of a person. Unconditional love is given for the fact that every human being is created in the image of God.

Love is also willing to suffer for what is right. We marvel at the news articles that share stories of people voluntarily choosing suffering for the good of another human being. A brother who gives a kidney to a dying sister, or a mother who gives bone marrow for a child's recovery all strike us because of their choices. But suffering love goes even deeper.

An intense love of another human being creates a willingness "to lay down one's life for a friend." I am convinced the Viet Nam War Memorial is moving not simply because of the sheer numbers of service men and women listed there. I believe we are moved beyond words because these soldiers knew the meaning of this intense love:

> O beautiful for heroes proved, in
> liberating strife;
> Who more than self their country loved,
> and mercy more than life.

The Apostle Paul wrote in AD 55 the supreme definition of love, whether it is for relationships or the mission in our lives. Paul said,

> Love is patient, love is kind. It does not
> envy, it does not boast, it is not proud. It is
> not rude, it is not self-seeking, it is not easily
> angered, it keeps no record of wrongs. Love
> does not delight in evil but rejoices in the
> truth. It always protects, always trusts,
> always hopes, always perseveres.

Transformational leadership, at its core essence, is love. If we intently lived no other quality than love, we would forever alter this planet.

• After reading Paul's statement about love, how could this type of love transform your relationships, organization or community? How would it transform you?

A Time for
Self-Reflection

*Leadership is an art: the first
responsibility of a leader is to define reality.
The last is to say "Thank you." In between,
the leader is a servant.*

—Max DePree
leadership expert & author

YOU HAVE COME FULL CIRCLE. In the Winter Season,
you began by defining reality—your reality. And in the
Autumn Season, you have found that leadership is saying
"Thank you" by demonstrating your belief in other people.
For they are only liberated by the consistency of your con-
victions, words and deeds.

And in between, I hope you have become a servant.
Through the Spring and Summer, I trust you have become a
continual learner as well as a liberator of other human
beings. Ultimately, I hope you have invited just one other
person to join you on this leadership journey.

As Bennis, DePree, Covey, Blanchard, Greenleaf and
others remind us, leadership is an art. There are no set rules,
guides or predetermining factors that will make you a leader.
Personal change or your willingness to lead doesn't come

from hacking at the leaves of attitude and behavior with quick-fix personality ethics techniques. Real change and effective leadership come from spending your waking hours planting, nurturing and tending to the life principles outlined in the *Four Seasons of Leadership*. As I hope you have discovered, leadership is an affair of the heart.

Your life legacy is to plant, water, nourish, raise and plant again these seeds of leadership until they mature within you, changing you from who you currently are into what you can become. Your family, the organization or community in which you live and work, as well as this planet, could receive no greater gift.

• Look back over the *Four Seasons of Leadership*. How have you changed? What has been the most influencing activity for you?

• Have you discovered ways of liberating others as well as inviting them on a leadership journey?

• Look ahead to the coming Winter. What have you left undone in this first adventure through the *Four Seasons of Leadership*? Are you living purposefully toward your mission?

• Do you feel your life is more focused and goal-directed than previously? Why or why not? If not, what will you do to make the changes necessary to become more focused?

Choose to Be Good Soil

A sower went out to sow his seed; and as he sowed, some fell along the path, and was trodden under foot, and the birds of the air devoured it. And some fell on the road; and as it grew up, it withered away, because it had no moisture. And some fell among thorns; and the thorns grew with it and choked it. And some fell into good soil and grew, and yielded a hundredfold. He who has ears let him hear.

—Jesus the Christ
The Bible, Luke 8:4-8

THROUGHOUT THIS BOOK, an invitation has been given to people of all ages, socioeconomic backgrounds, ethnic or racial groups to internally plant and nurture the seeds of purpose, character and leadership. There is also an invitation to realize that all planting and growth is not about a quick fix but that real personal development happens over your lifetime. The real point about all life and leadership is understanding that it is not about a position one holds, but about who you are inside.

For decades, we have confused leadership with those in positions of power or those who wear a hierarchical mantle bestowed on them. But the essence of true leadership is eloquently captured in the words of William Pollard, who writes,

> *Will the leader stand up? Not the president, or the person with the most distinguished title, but the role model. Not the highest paid person in the group, but the risk taker. Not the person with the largest car or the biggest home, but the servant. Not the person who promotes himself or herself, but the promoter of others. Not the administrator, but the initiator. Not the taker, but the giver. Not the talker, but the listener.*

The role of leader is not for the faint-hearted or for those who want the opportunity for a while or at least until too much is personally required of them. Transforming leadership comes only when we admit our inadequacies, then commit ourselves to intense work for correcting them. In the end, if you are committed and willing to cheerfully labor, with a glad heart, planting where you may find thistles or may never harvest, you are prepared to undertake the journey of leadership.

I have spent many years teaching in the college classroom and through seminars around this country. I am reminded each time I stand before an audience that learning, leadership and change are ultimately a personal choice. I am also quite aware that only a handful of people in the crowd will take the message, gently tuck it into the fertile soil of their hearts and make the commitment to the hard work of personal growth.

My hope is that while reading *The Four Seasons of Leadership* you have taken these kernels of wisdom and planted them in your heart. And if you are persistent and focused during these Seasons, I am convinced these seeds will multiply a hundred times what you have sown.